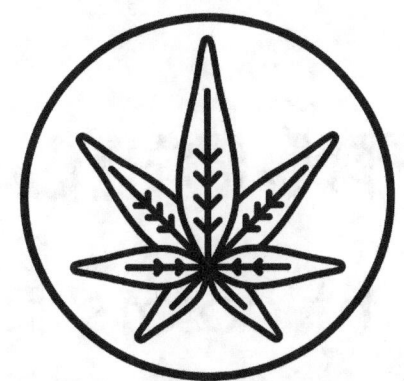

# STAY HIGH, STAY RELAXED

*Coloring book for Cannabidiols explorer*

## This book belongs to

..................................................

..................................................

..................................................

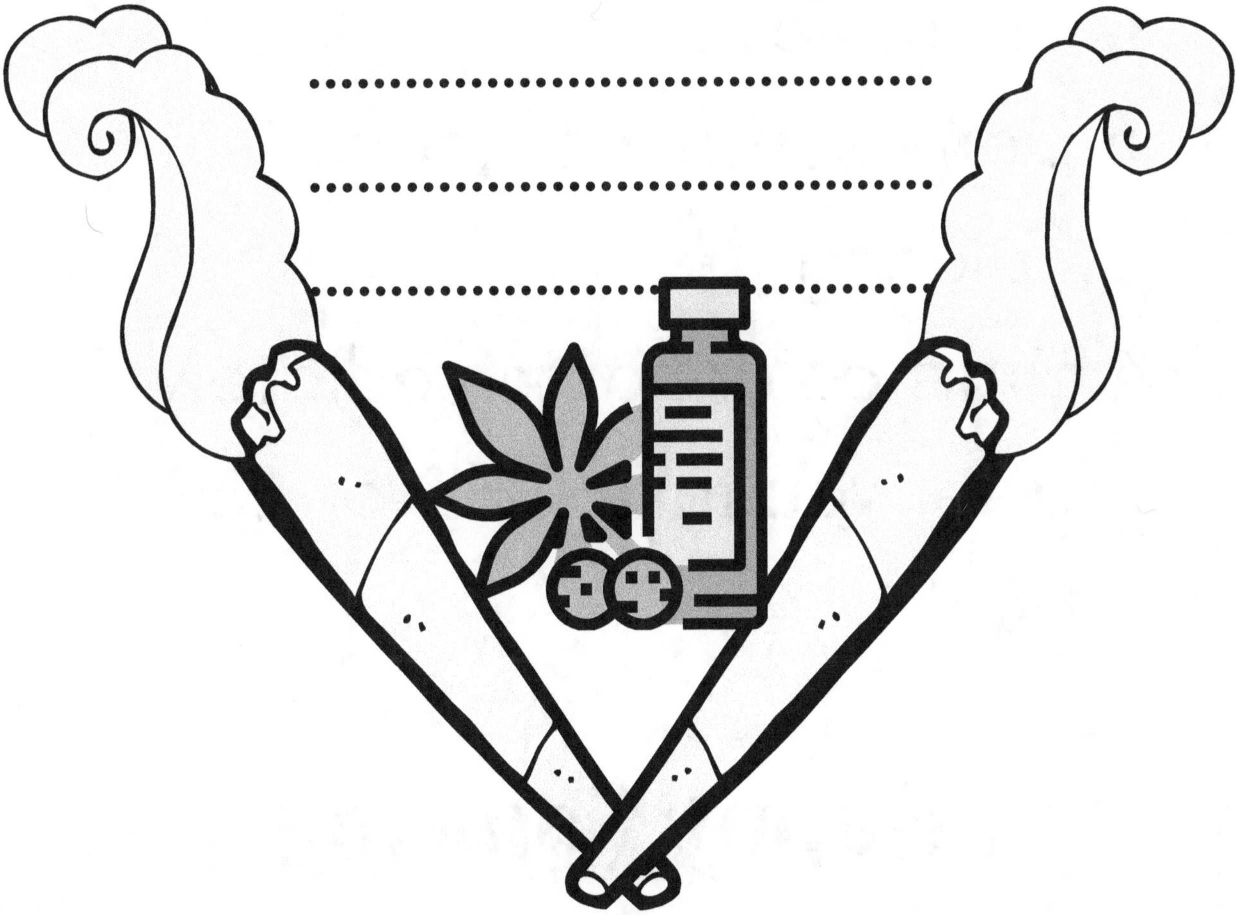

# INSTRUCTIONS

1. Use bright colors to intensify optical illusion while you are high or on trip.
2. Use color pencils for better outcome
3. Don't complain, keep coloring.
4. Start coloring immediately after you take CBD or any acid.

*Happy Coloring*

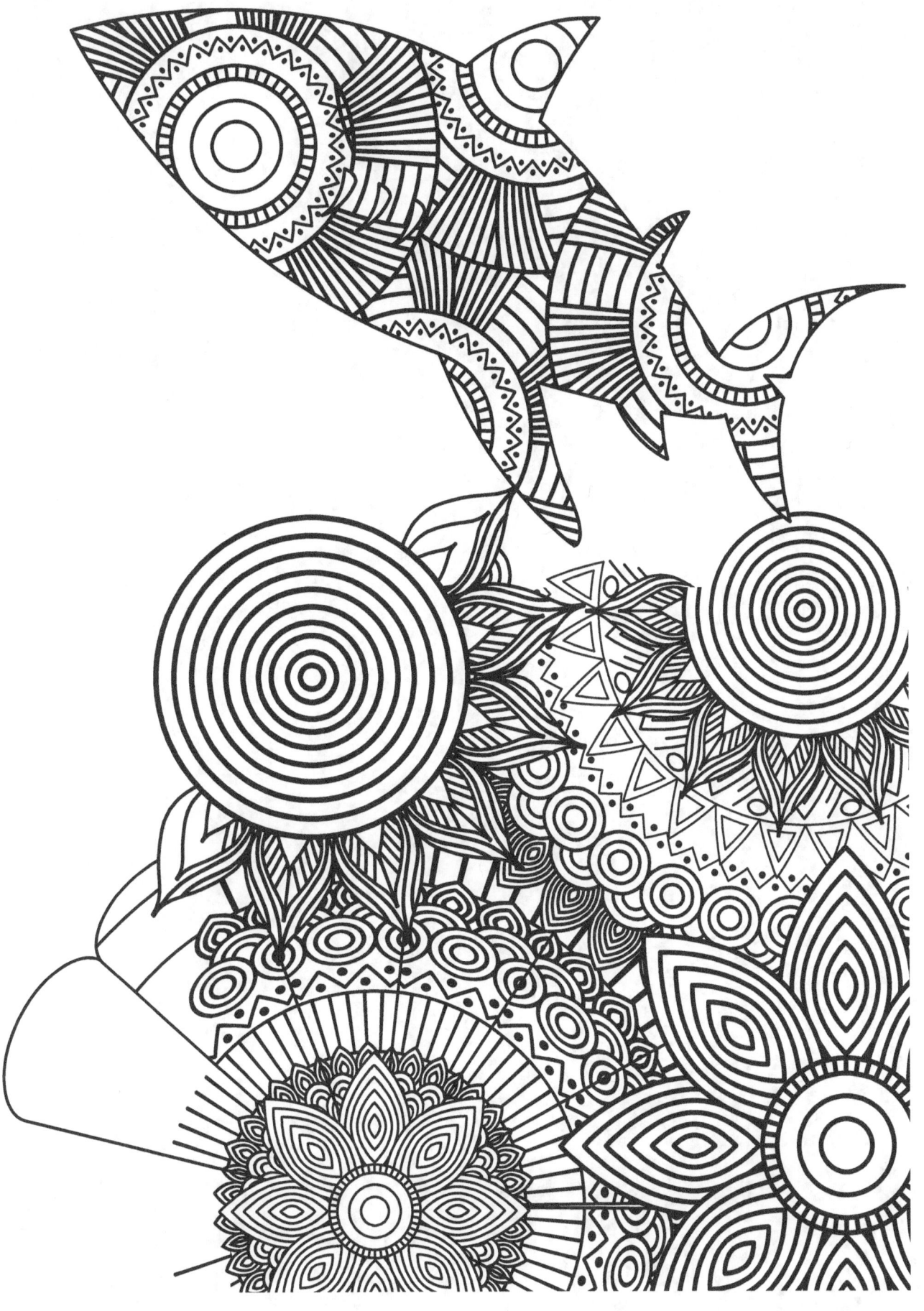

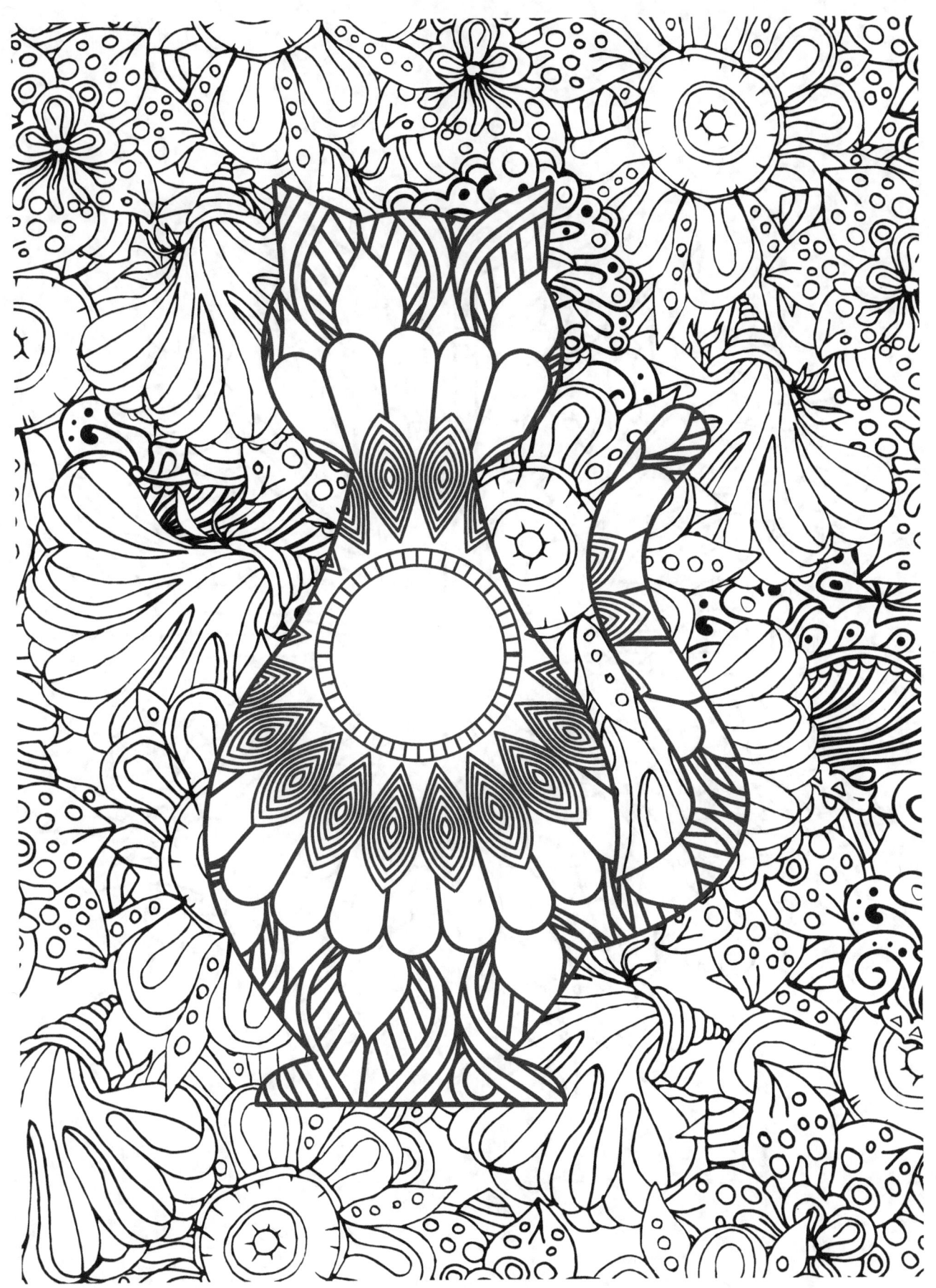

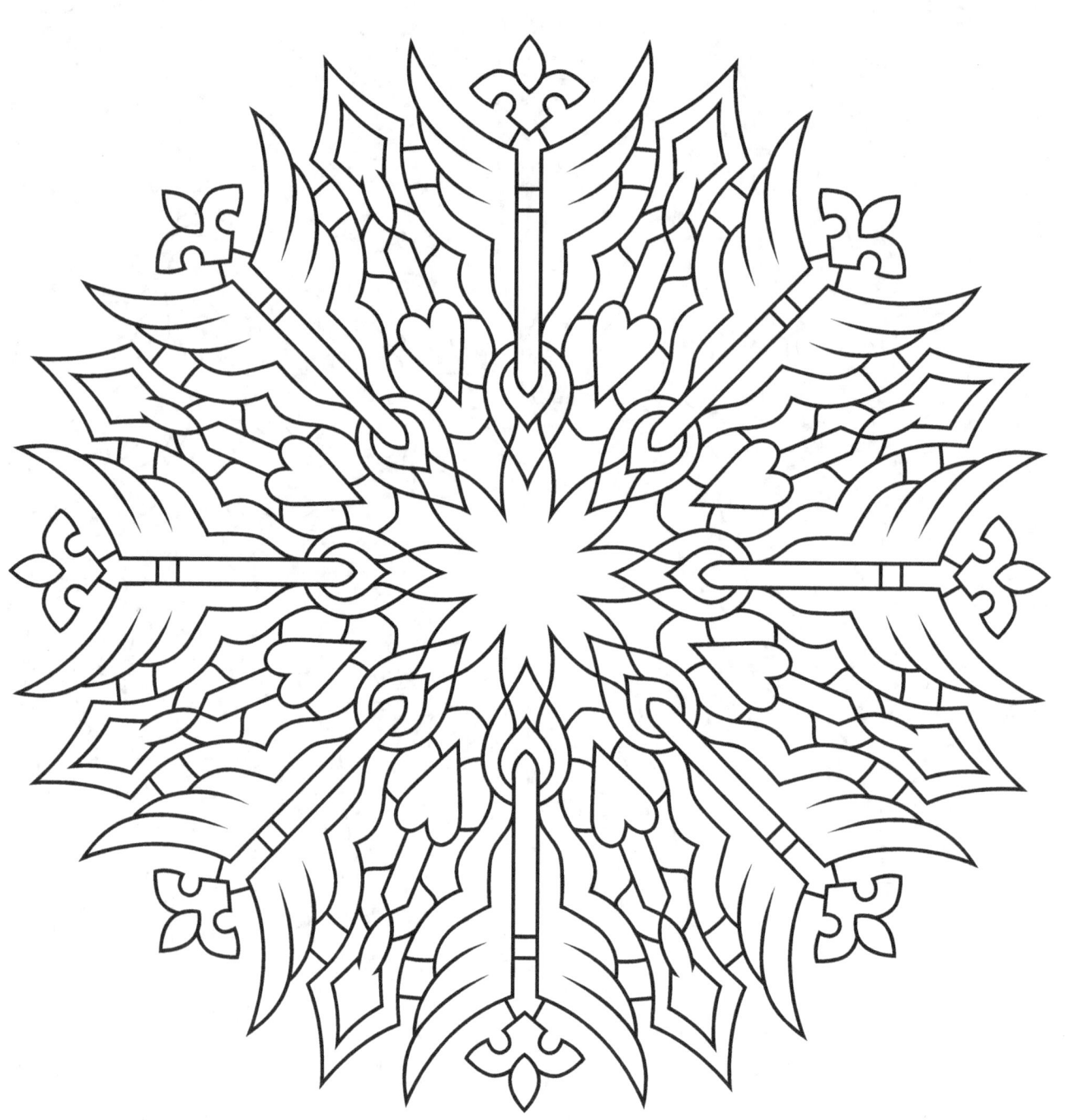

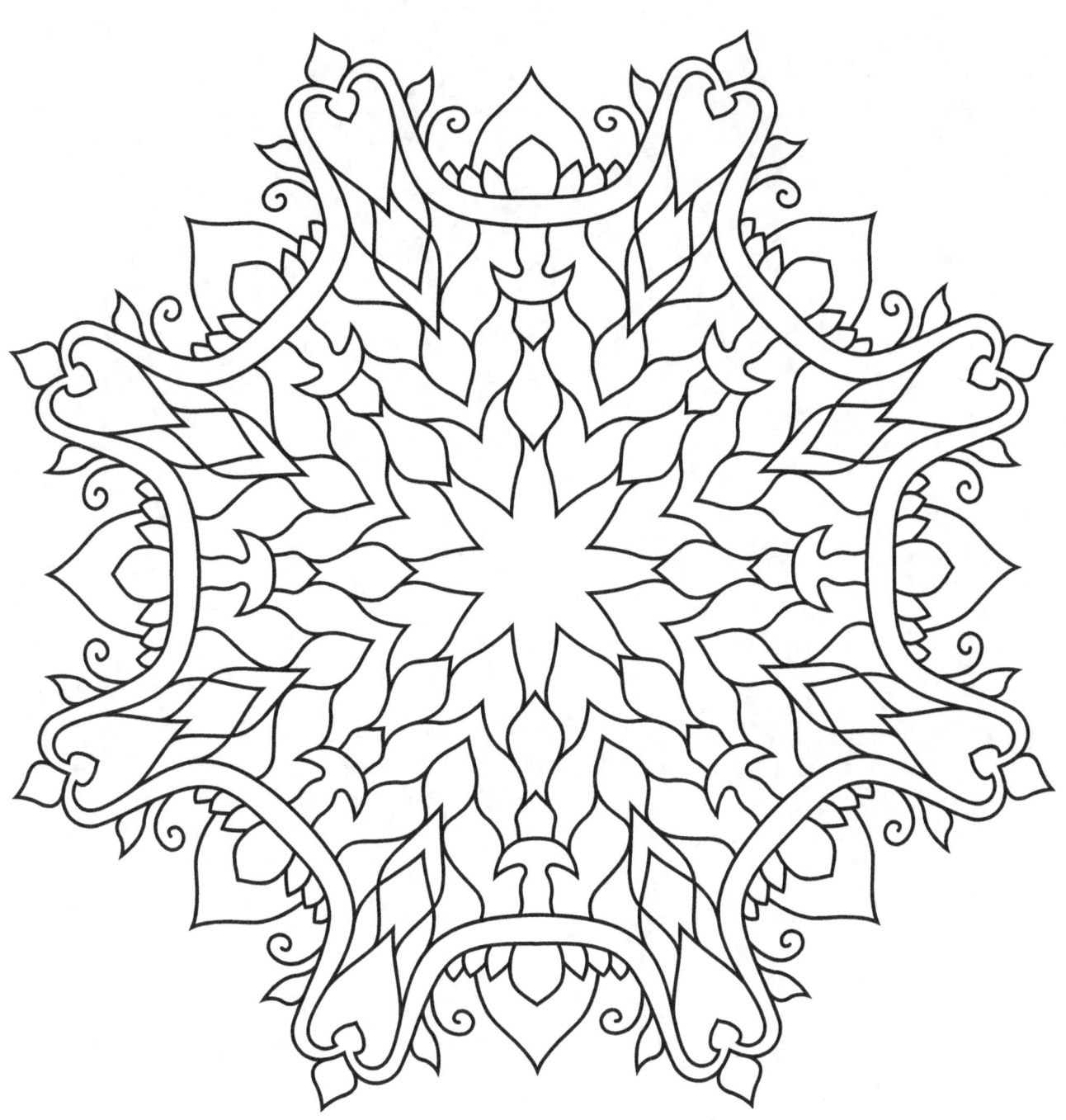

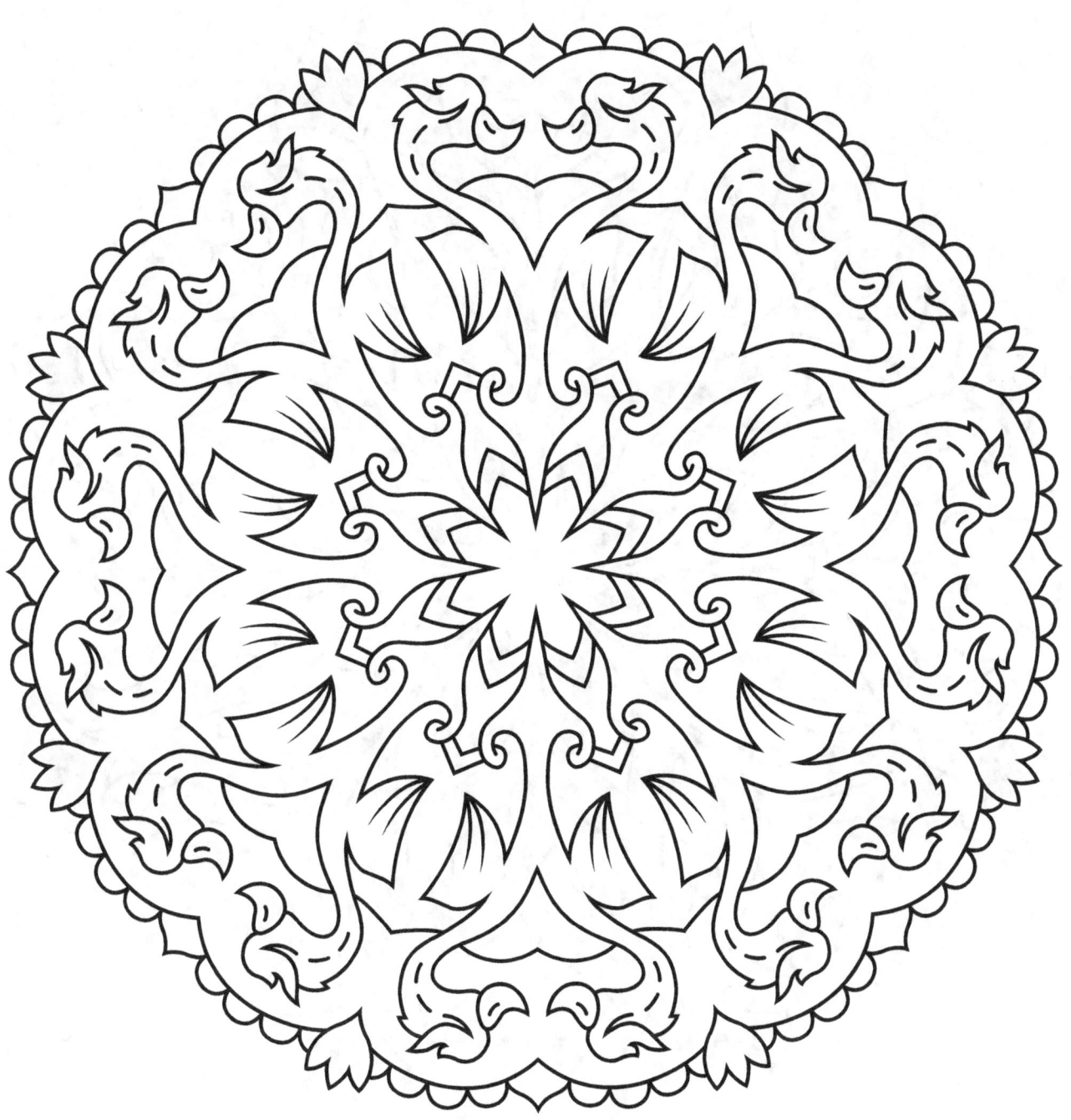

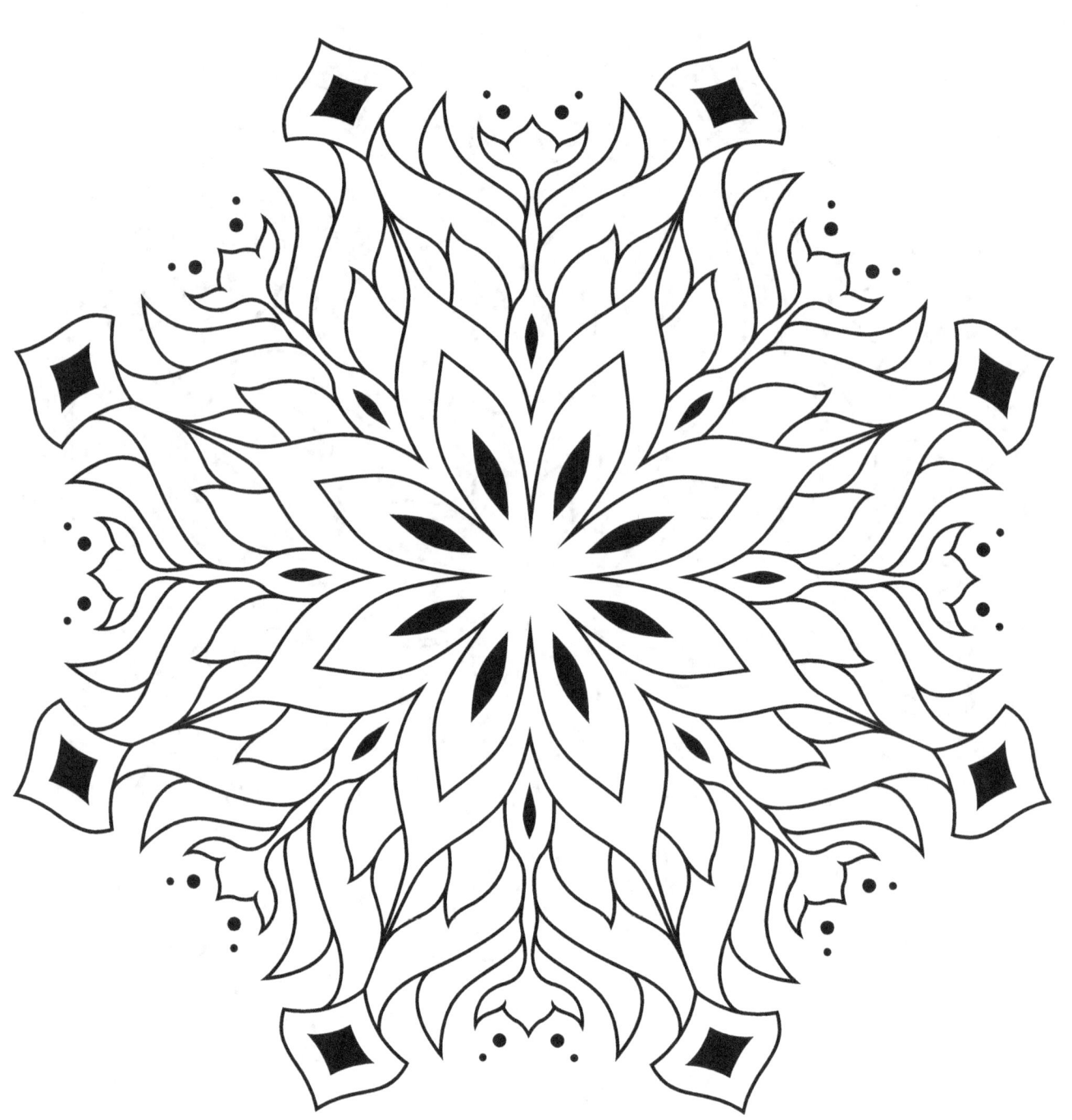

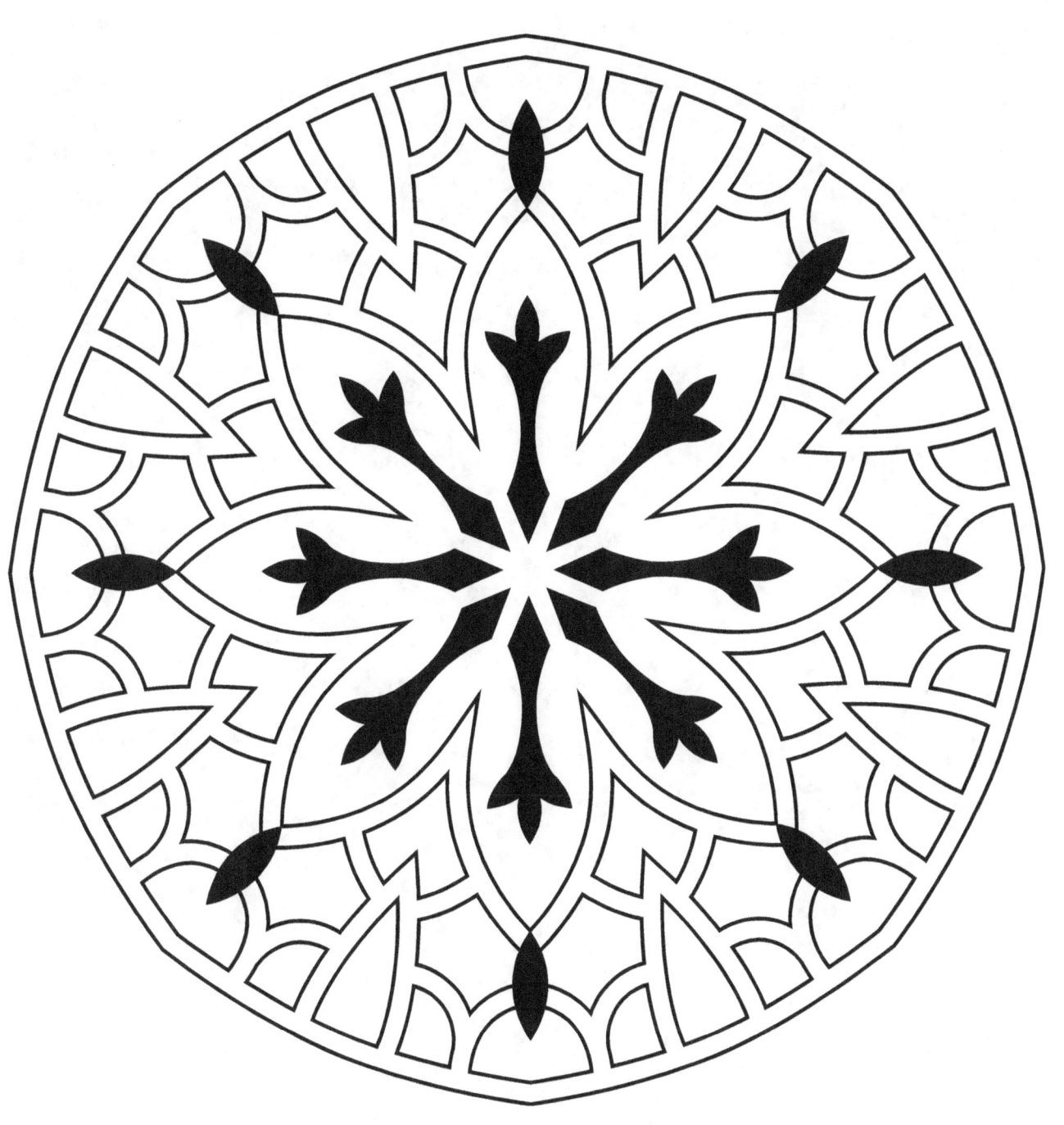

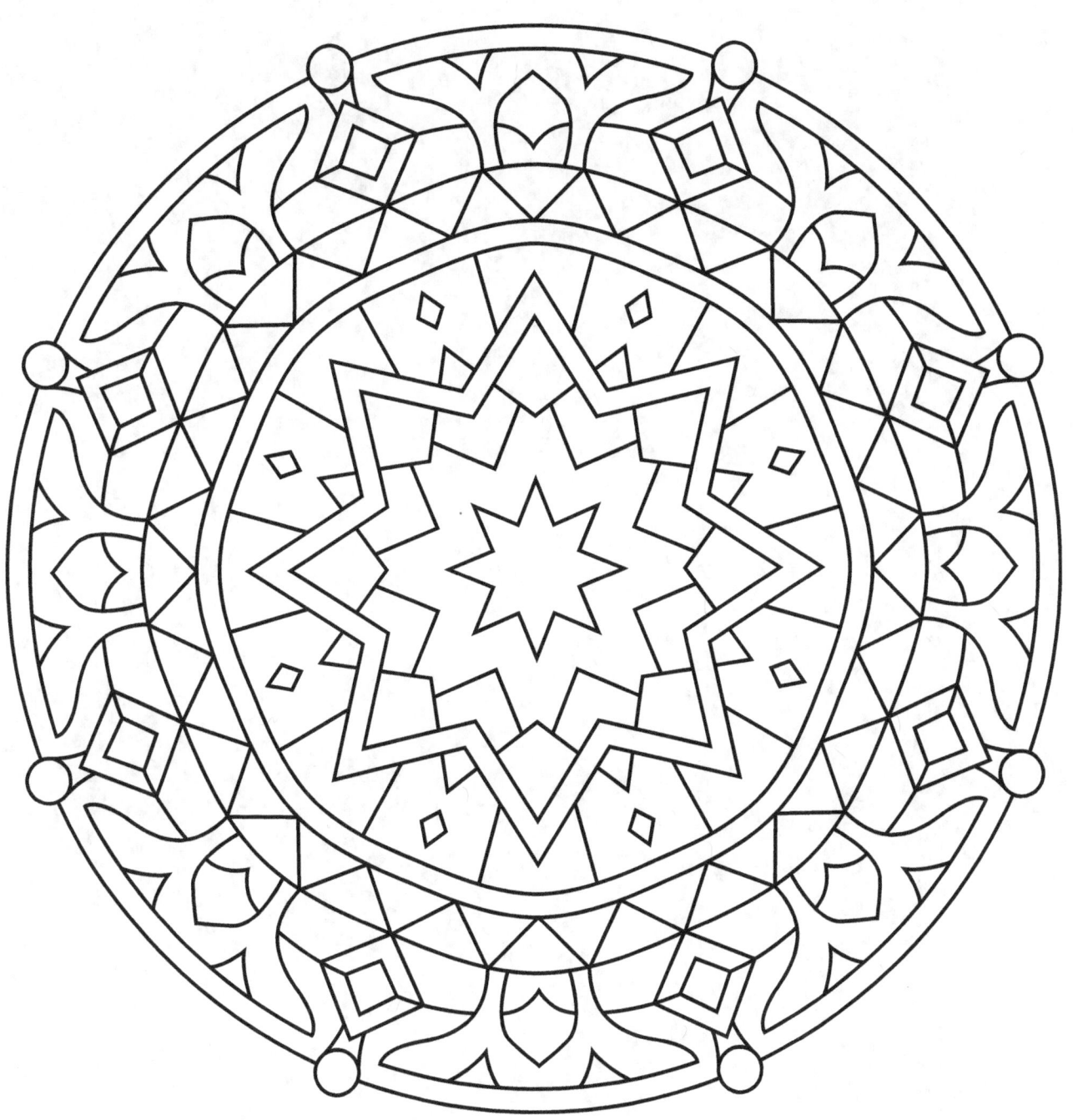

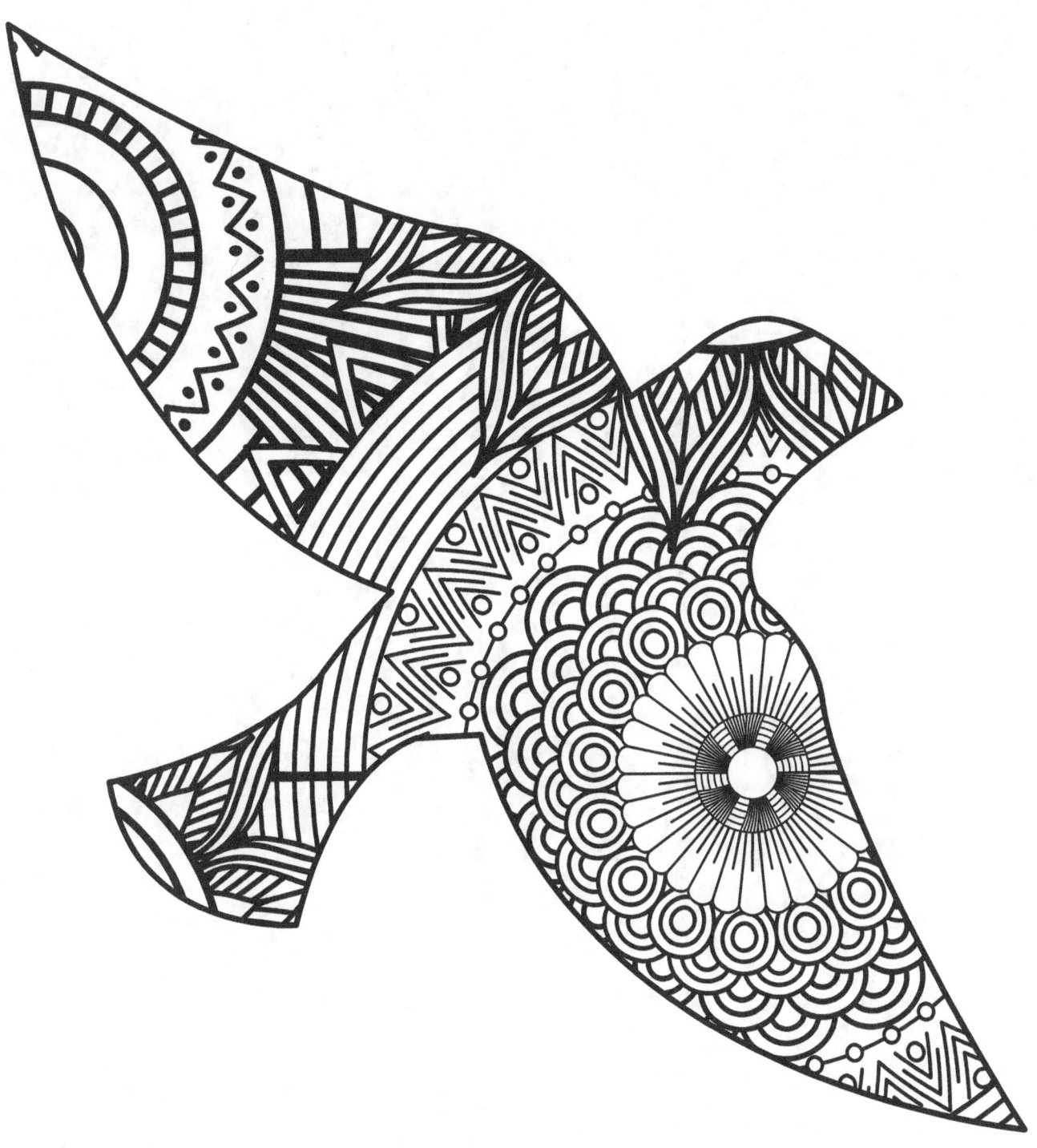

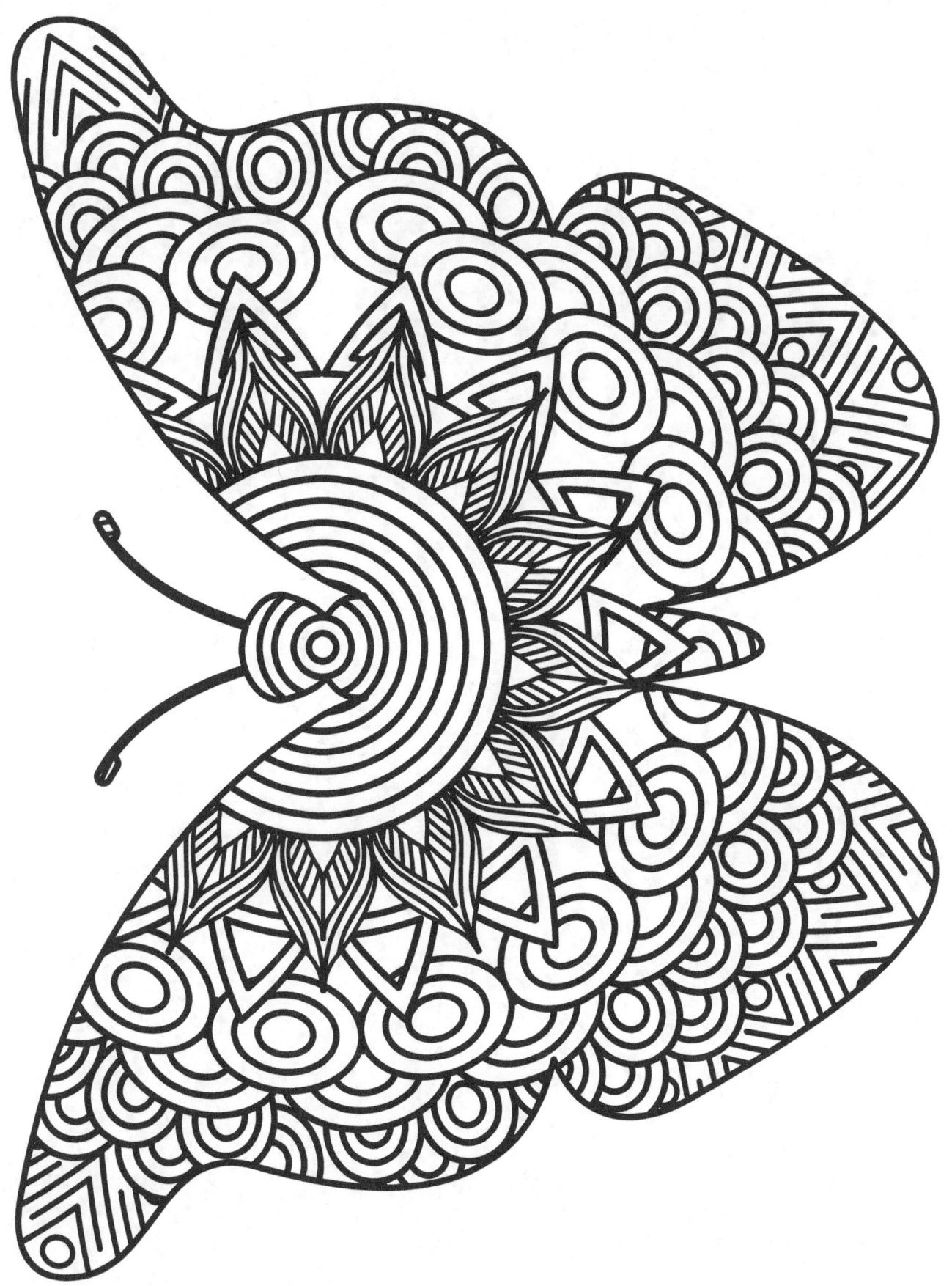

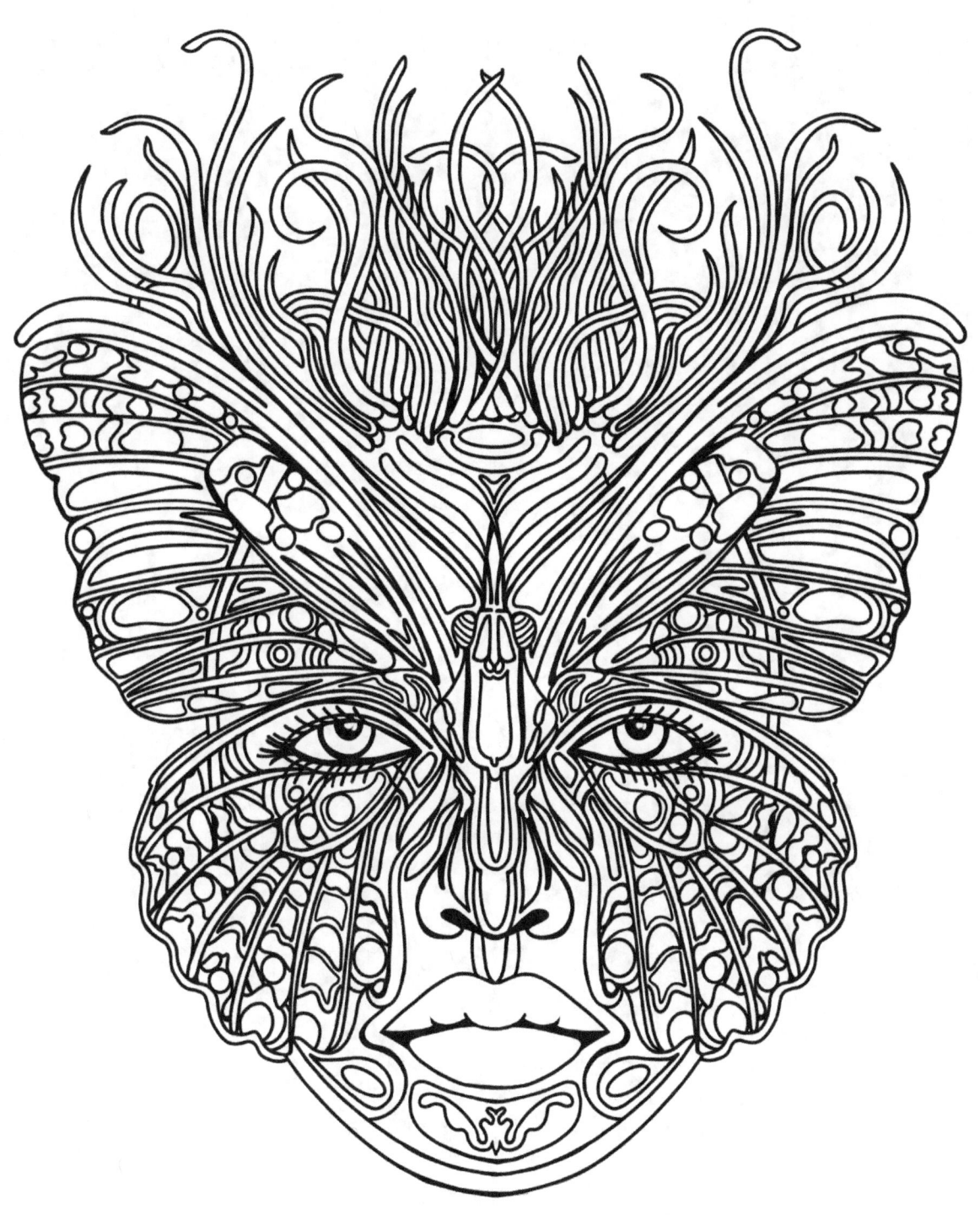

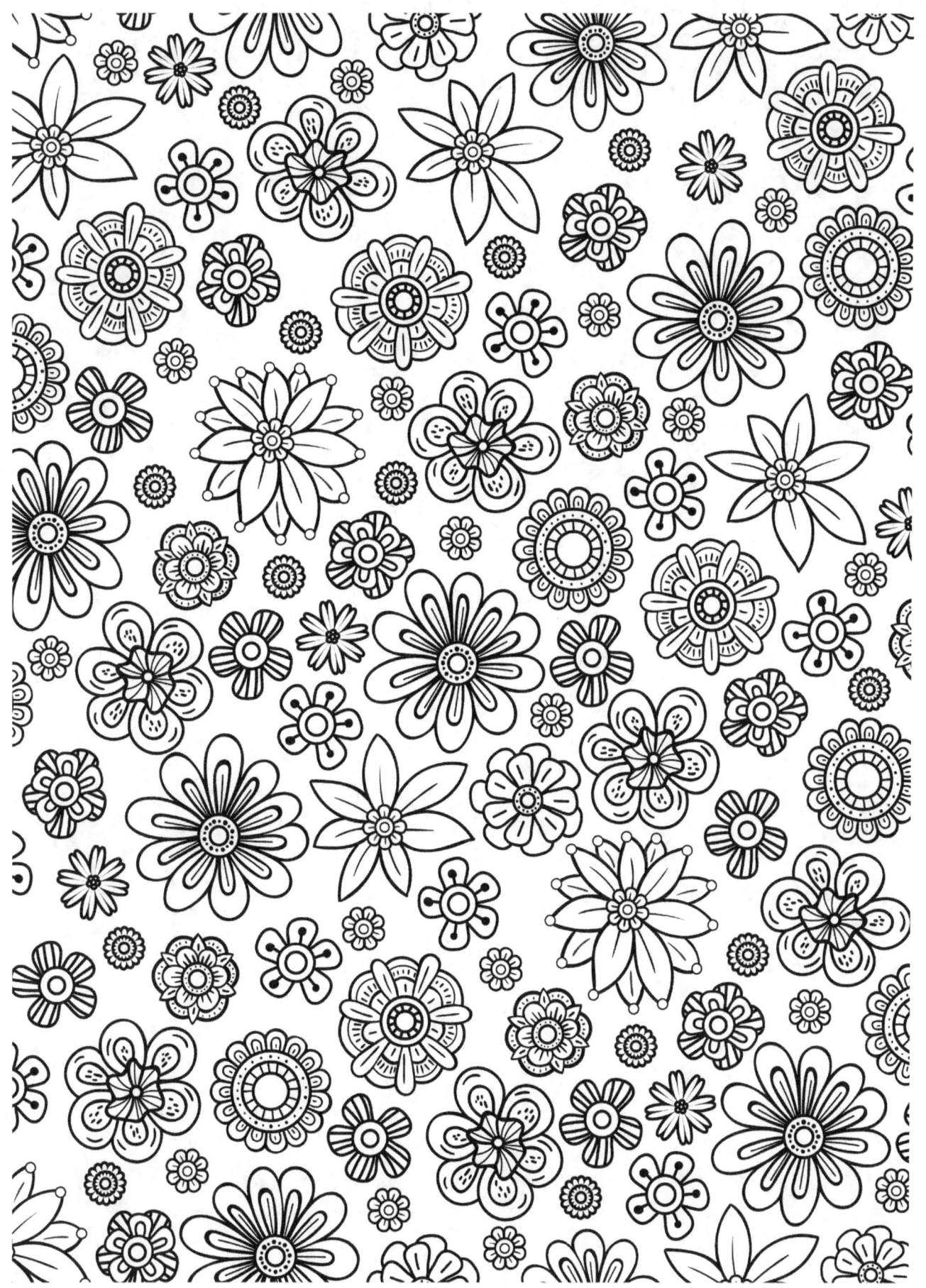

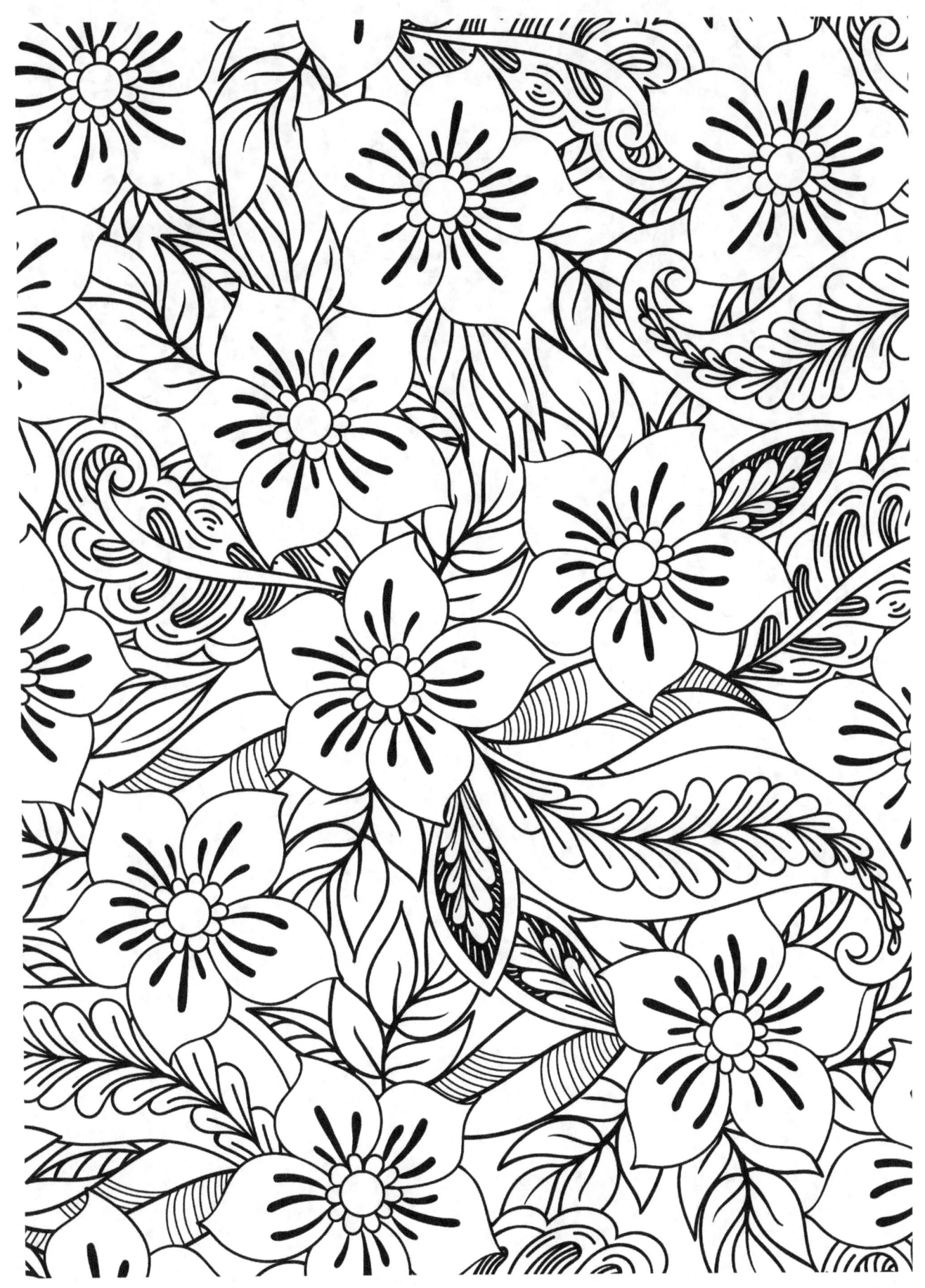

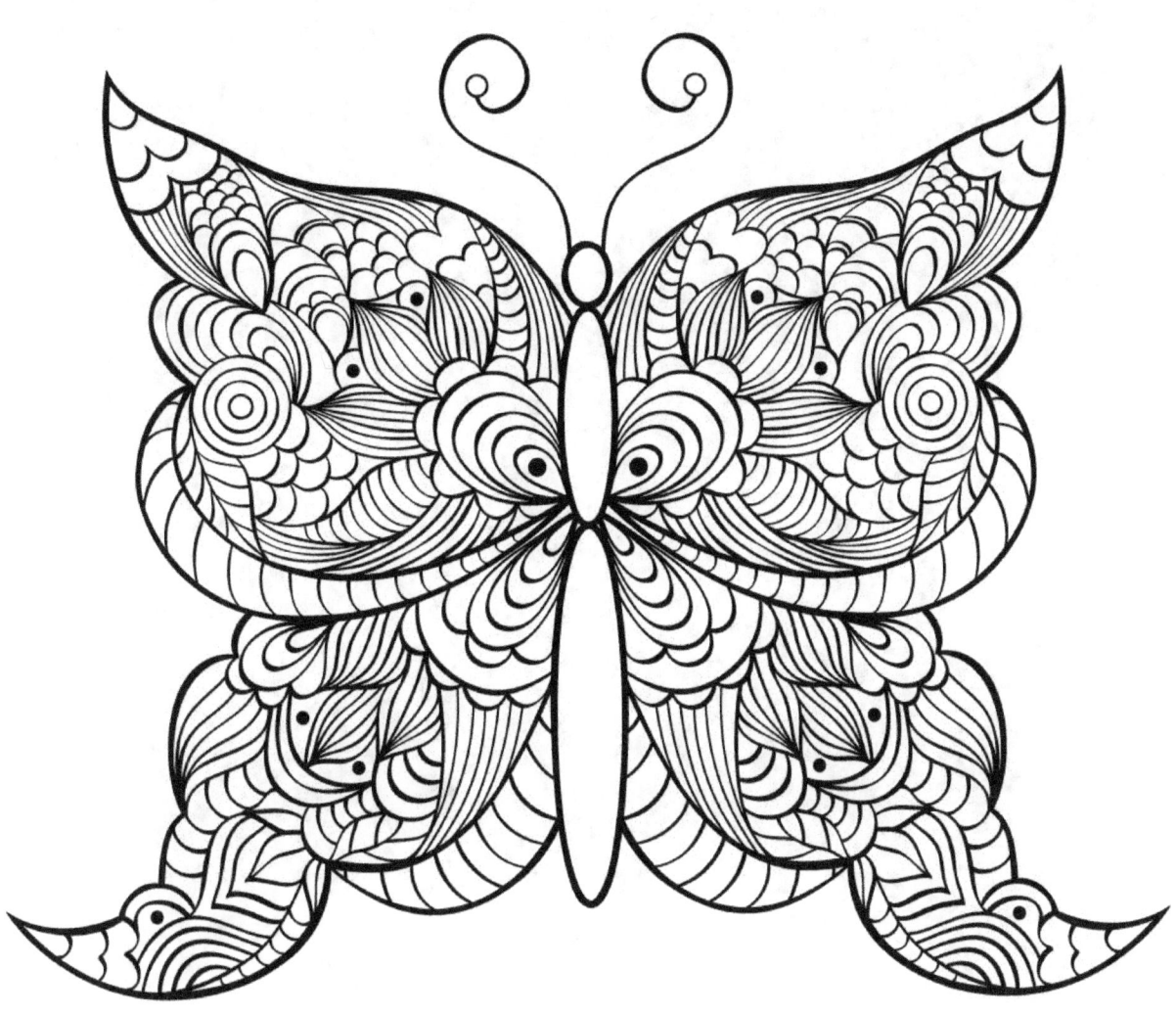

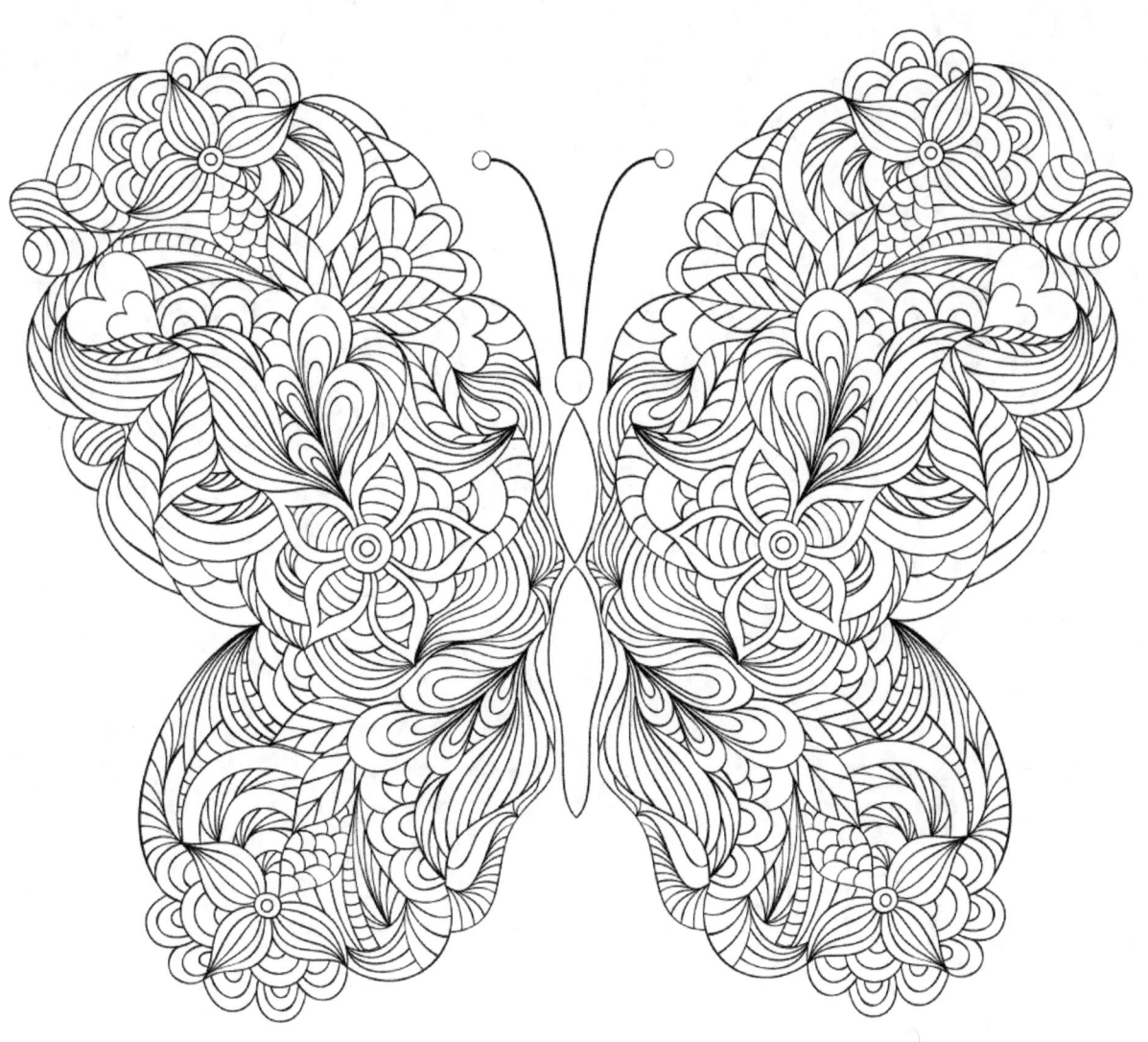

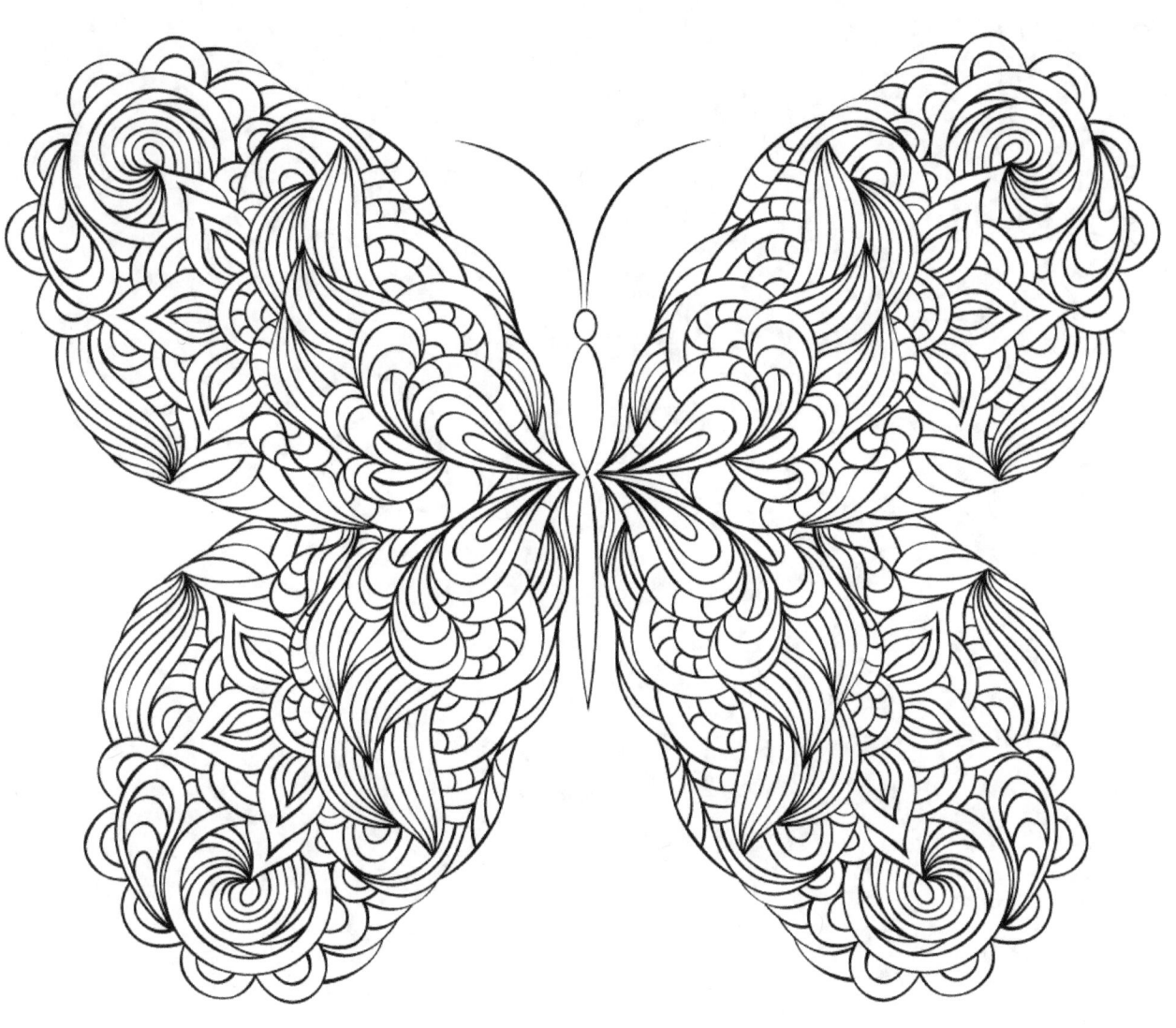

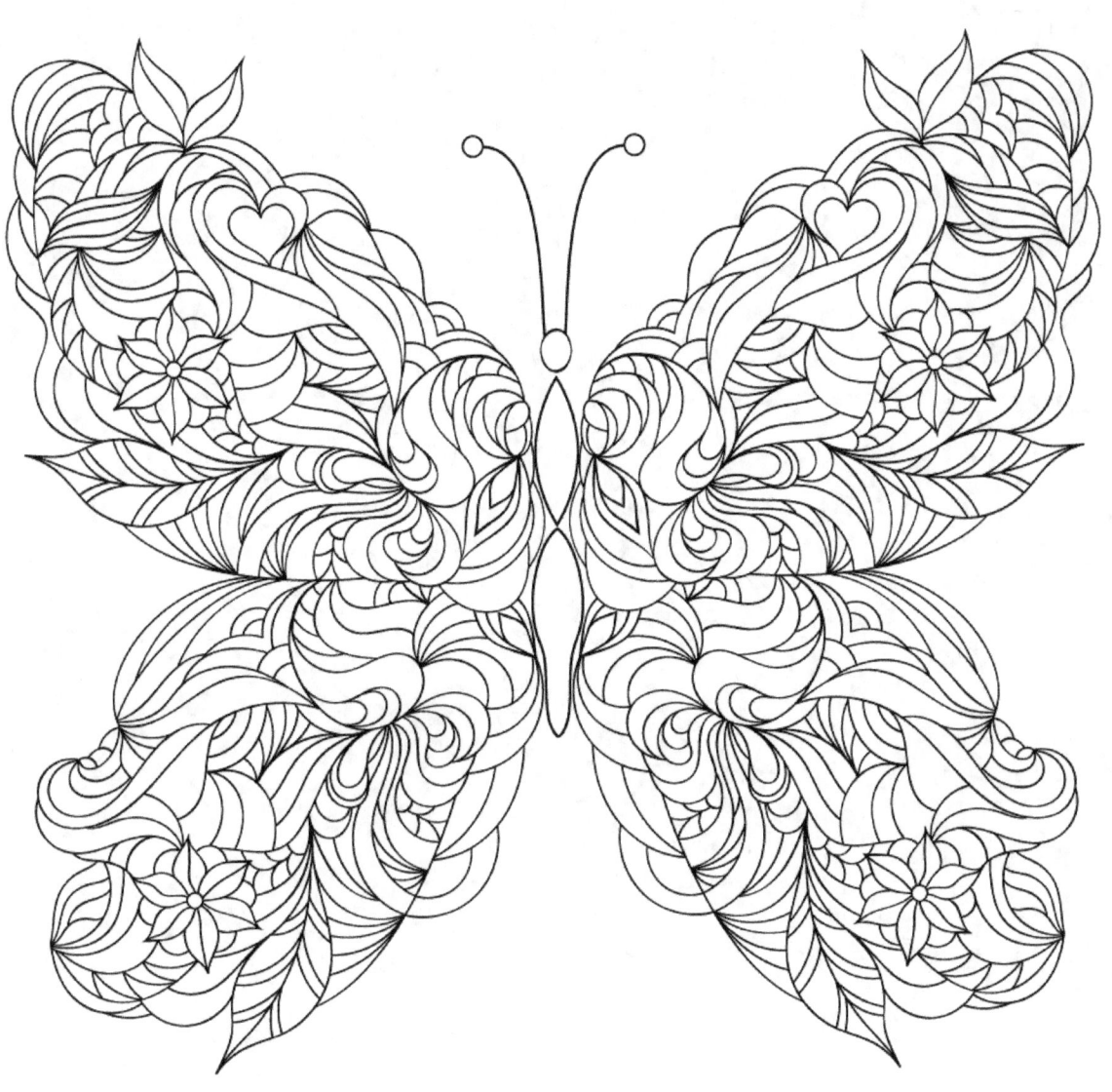

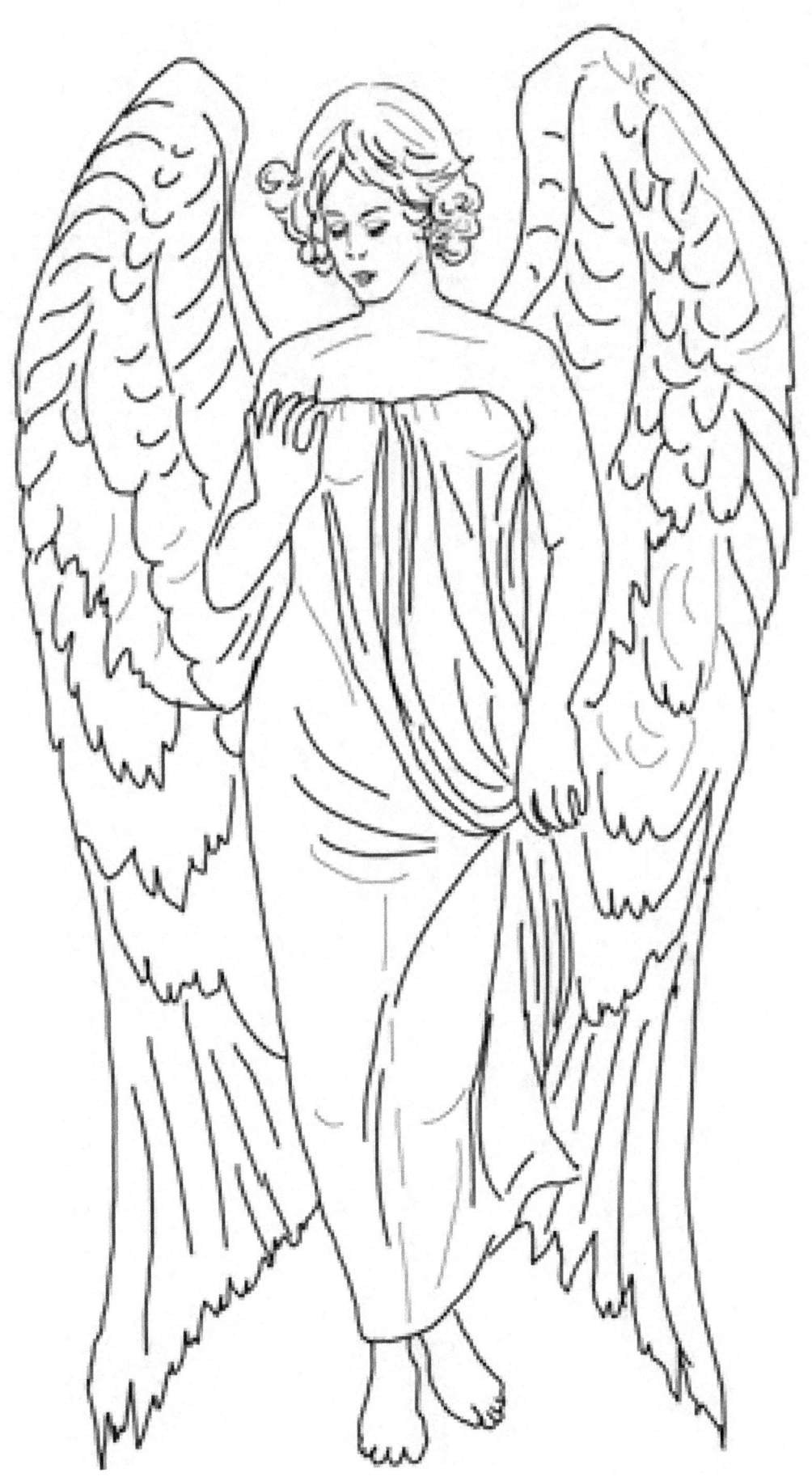

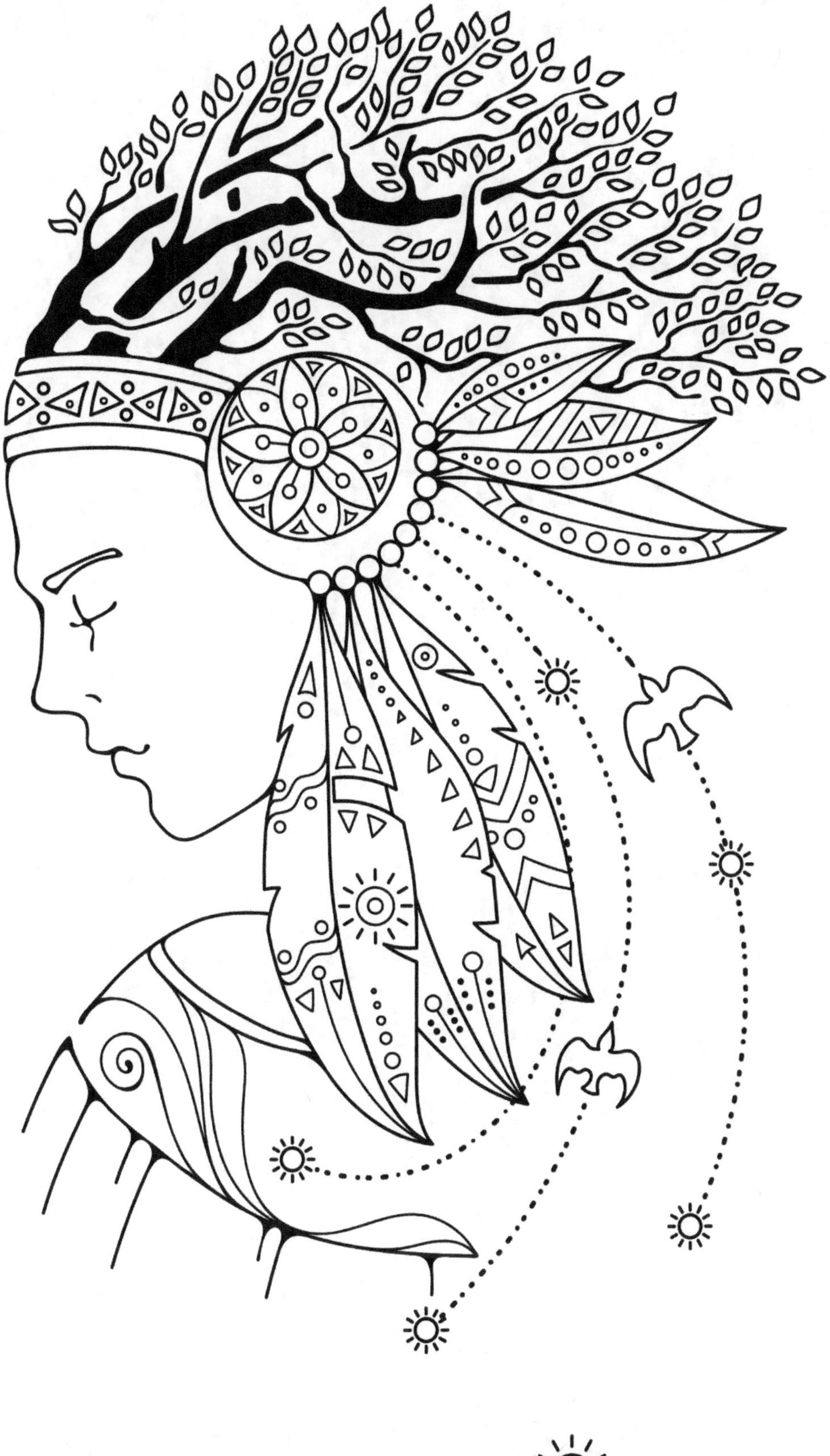

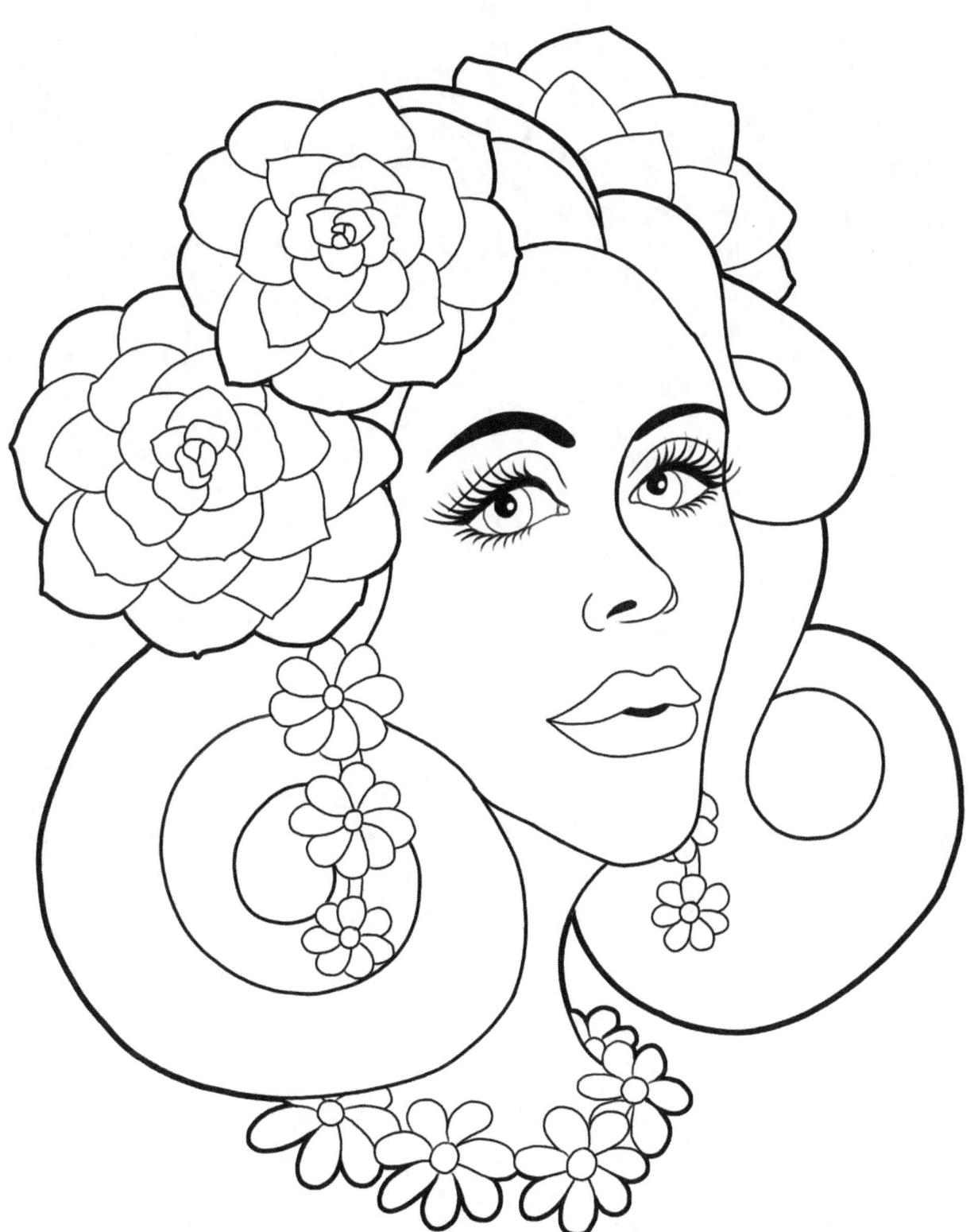

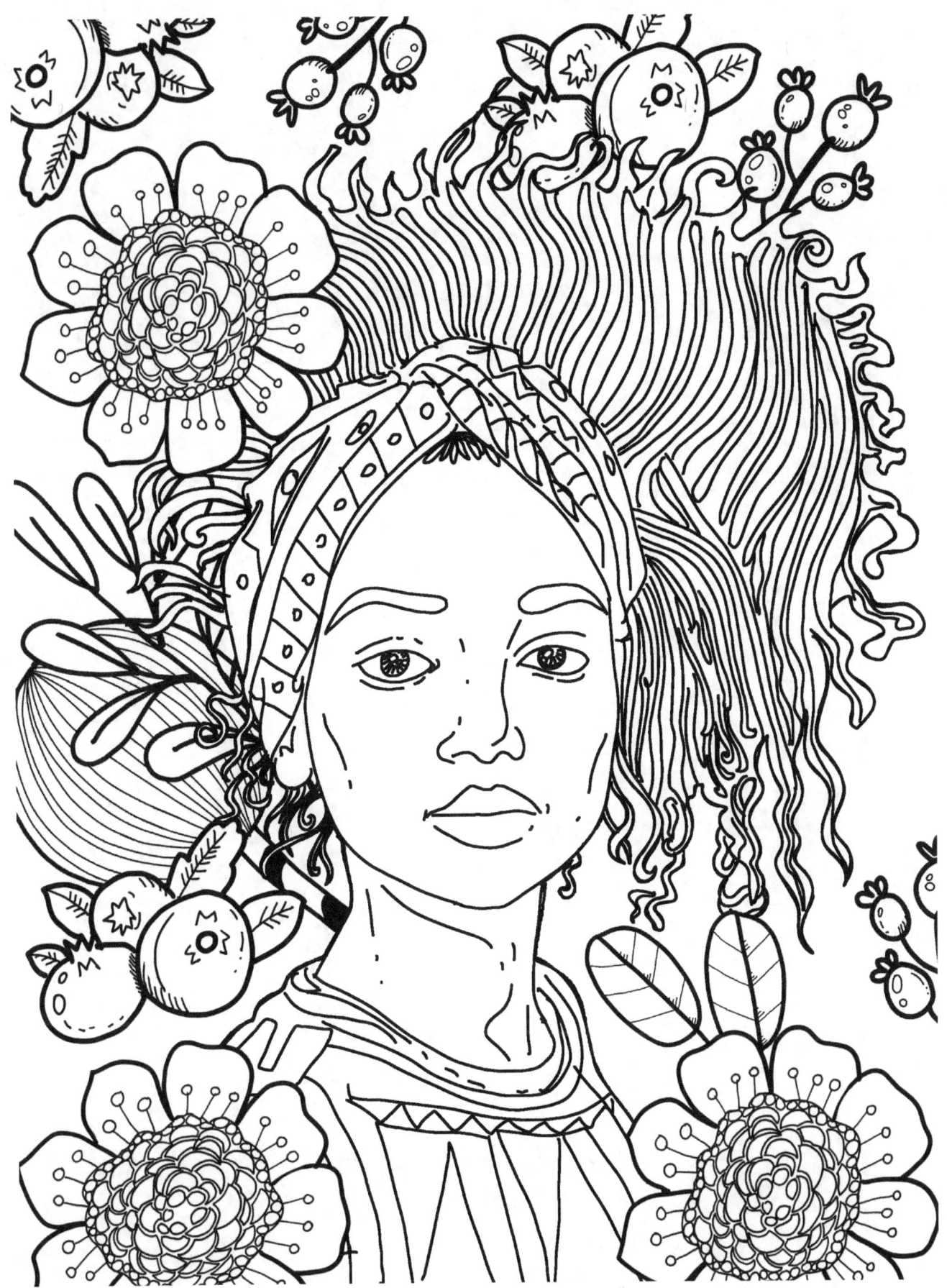

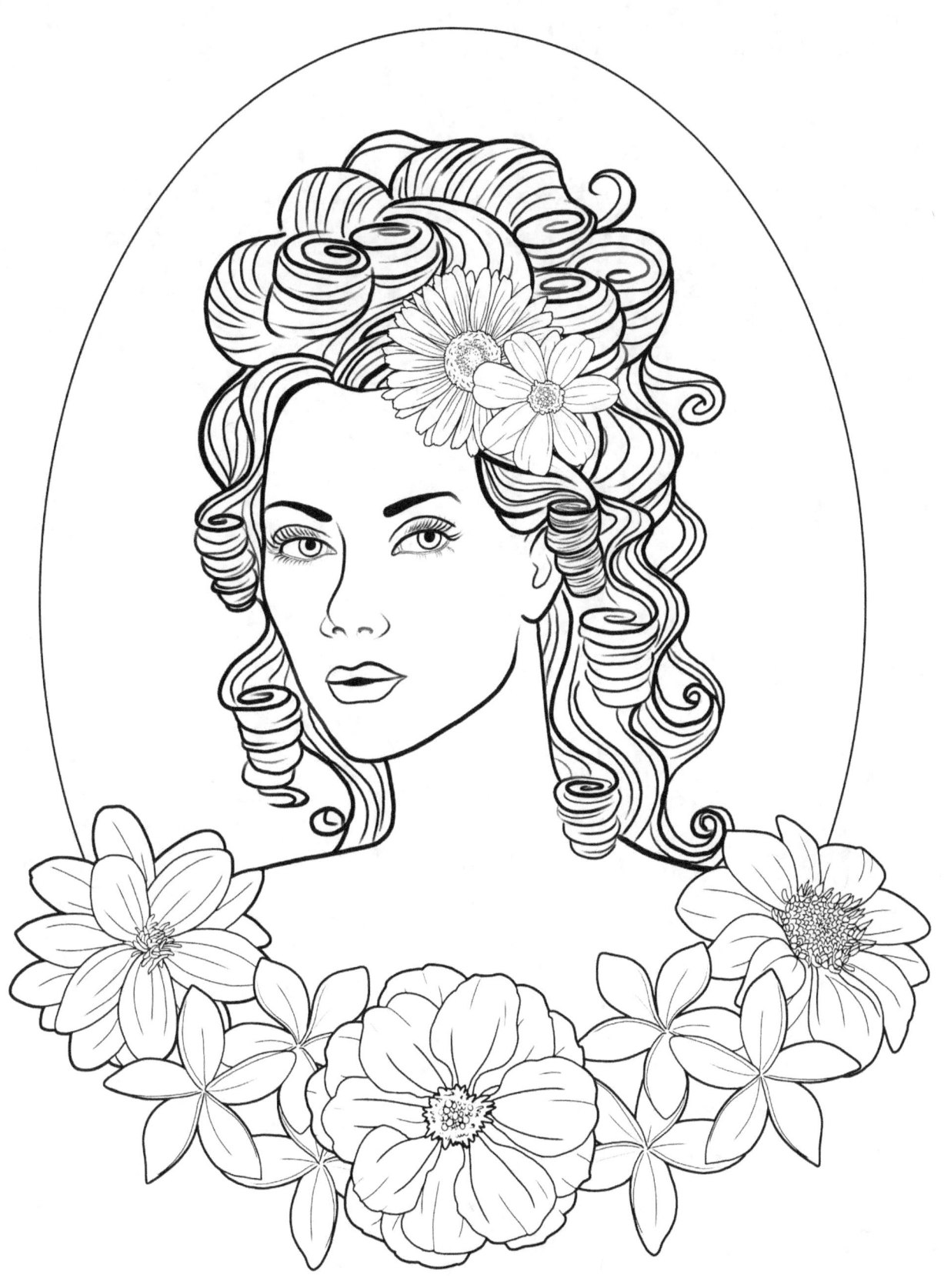

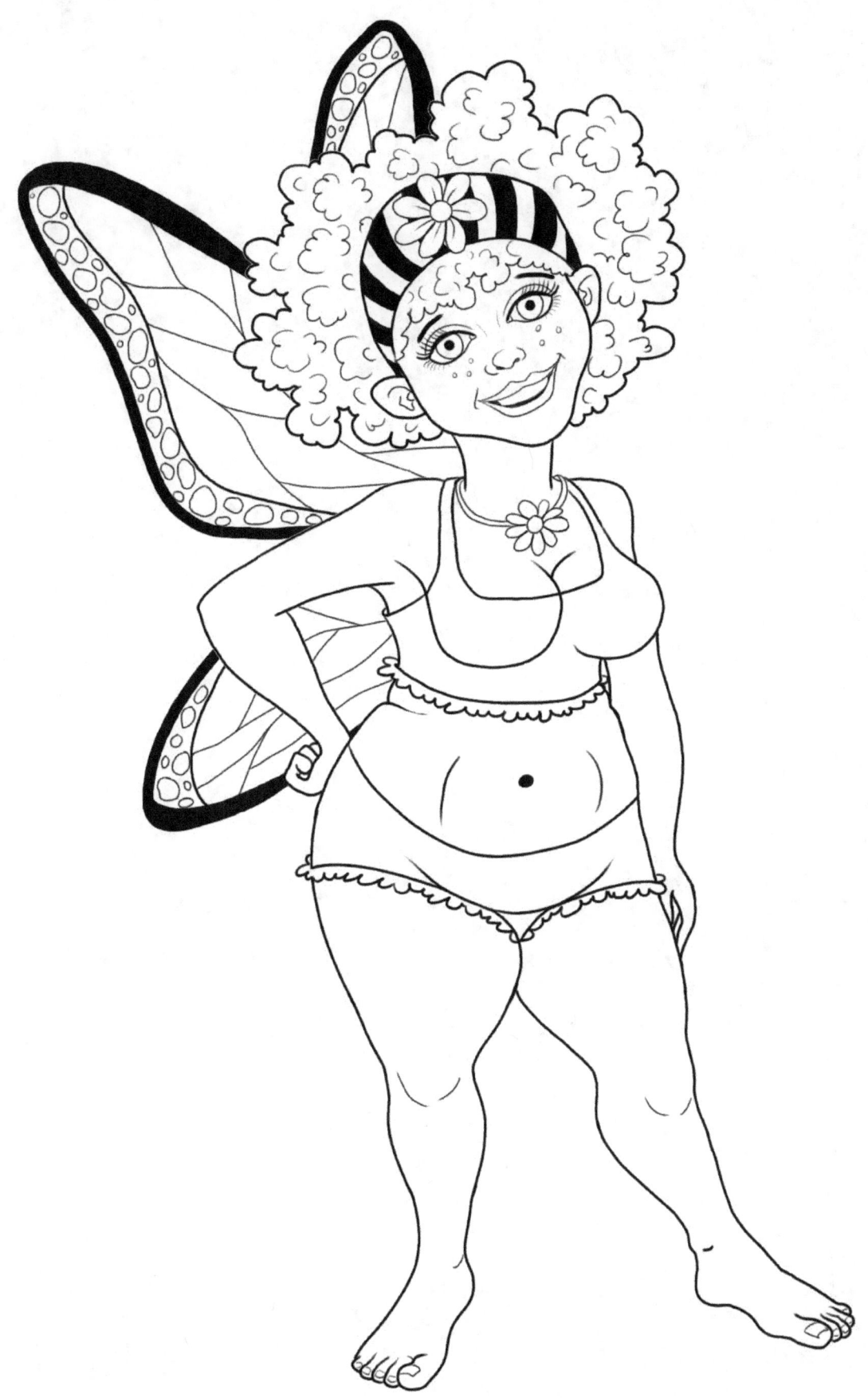

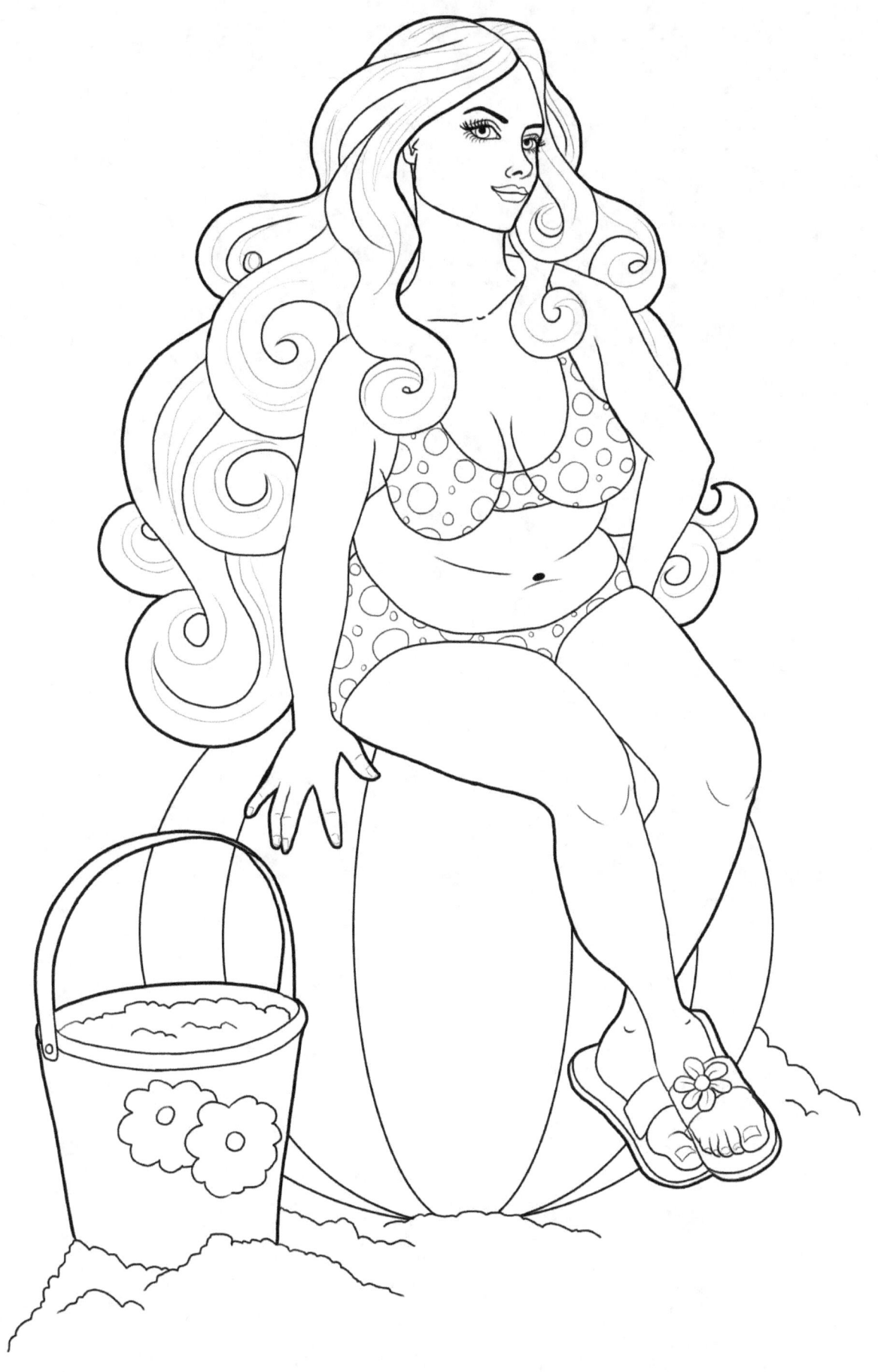

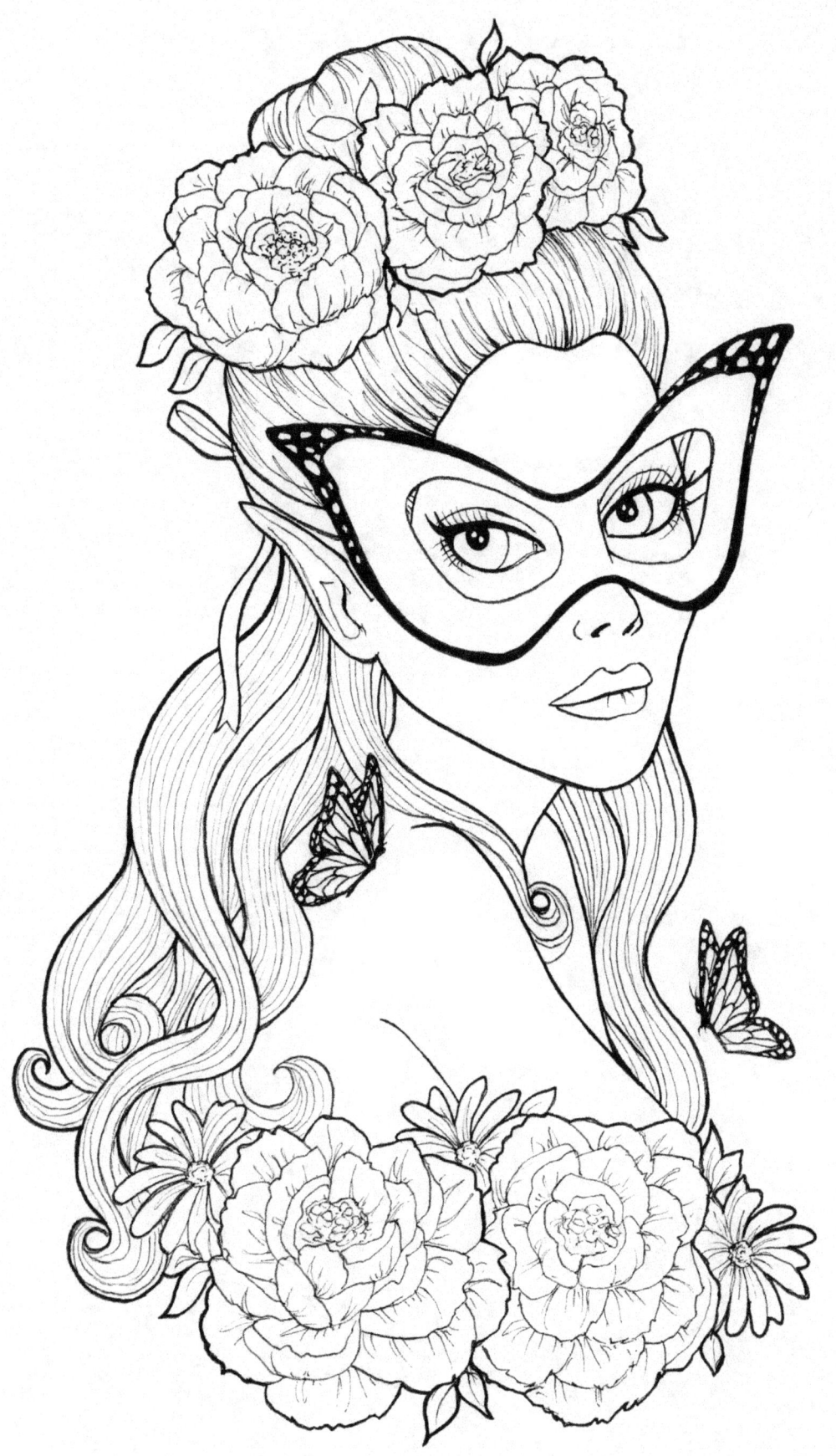

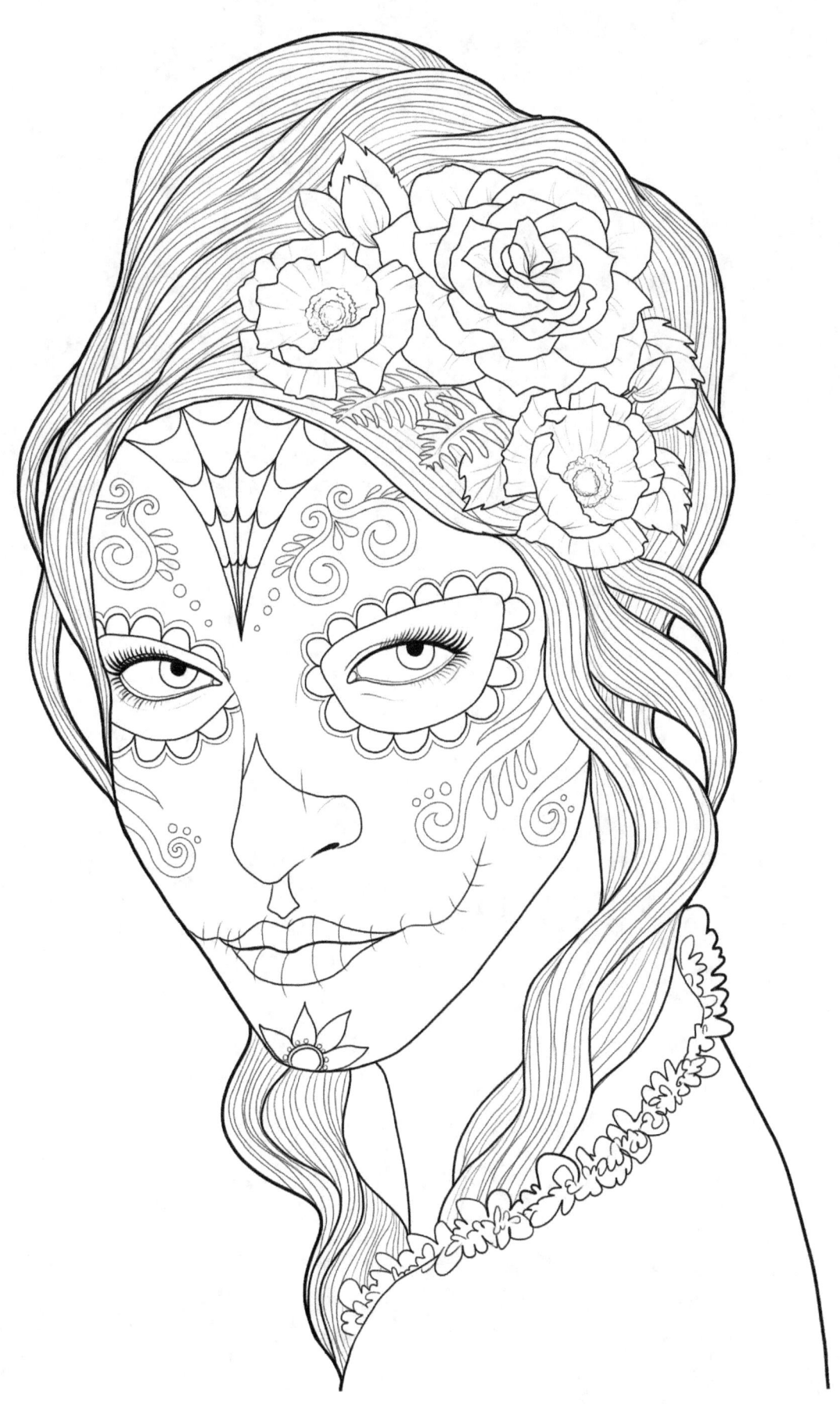

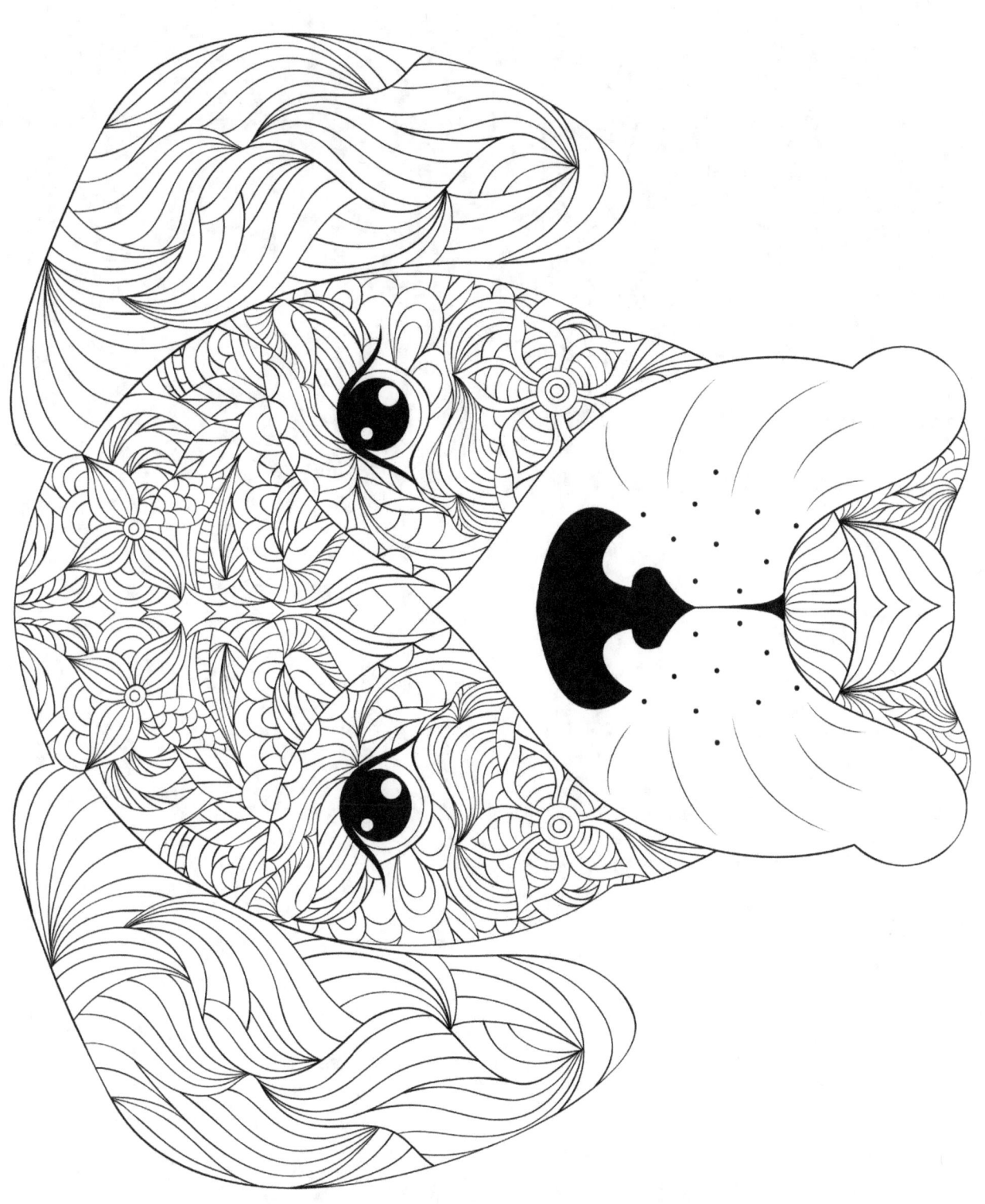

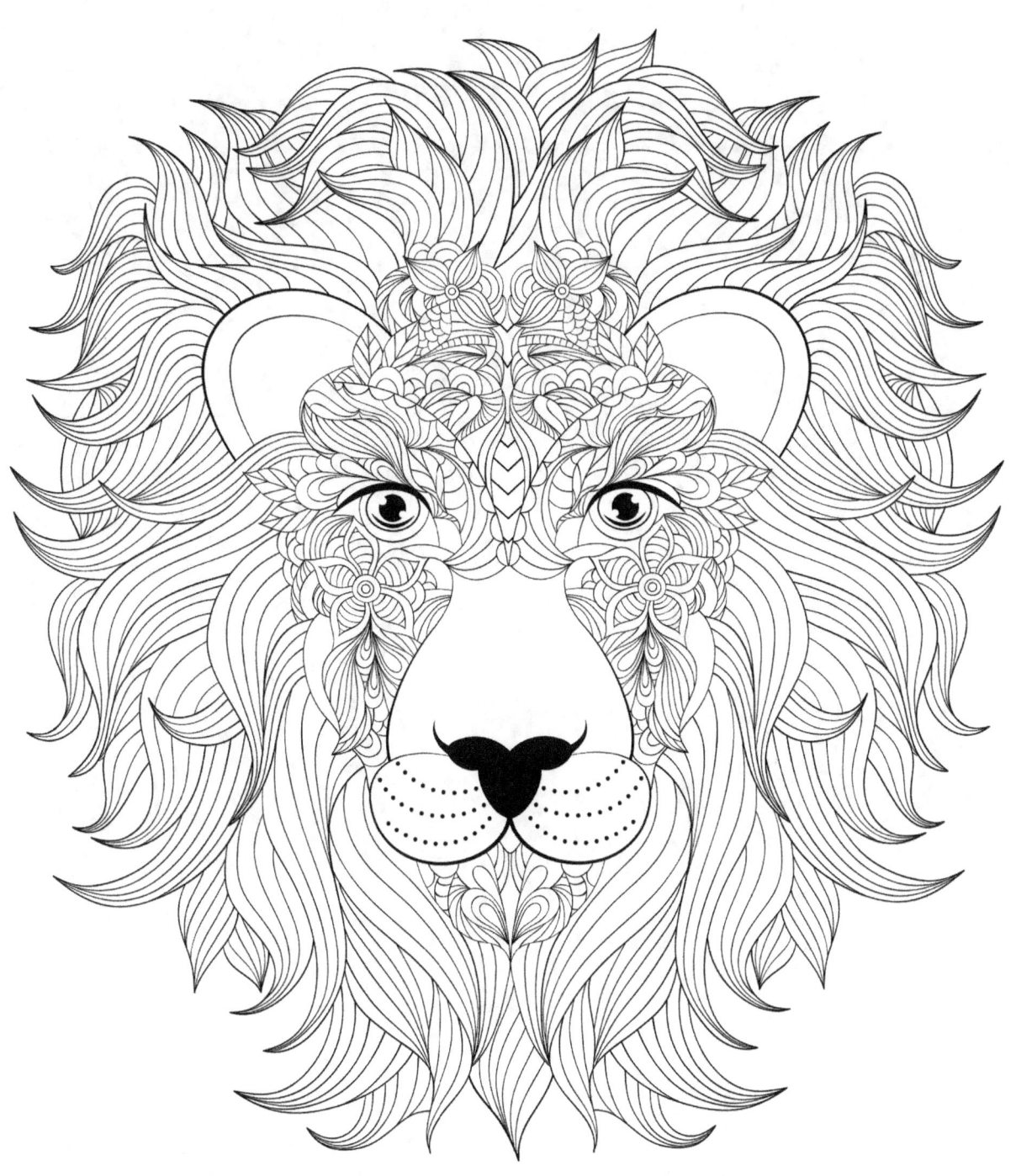

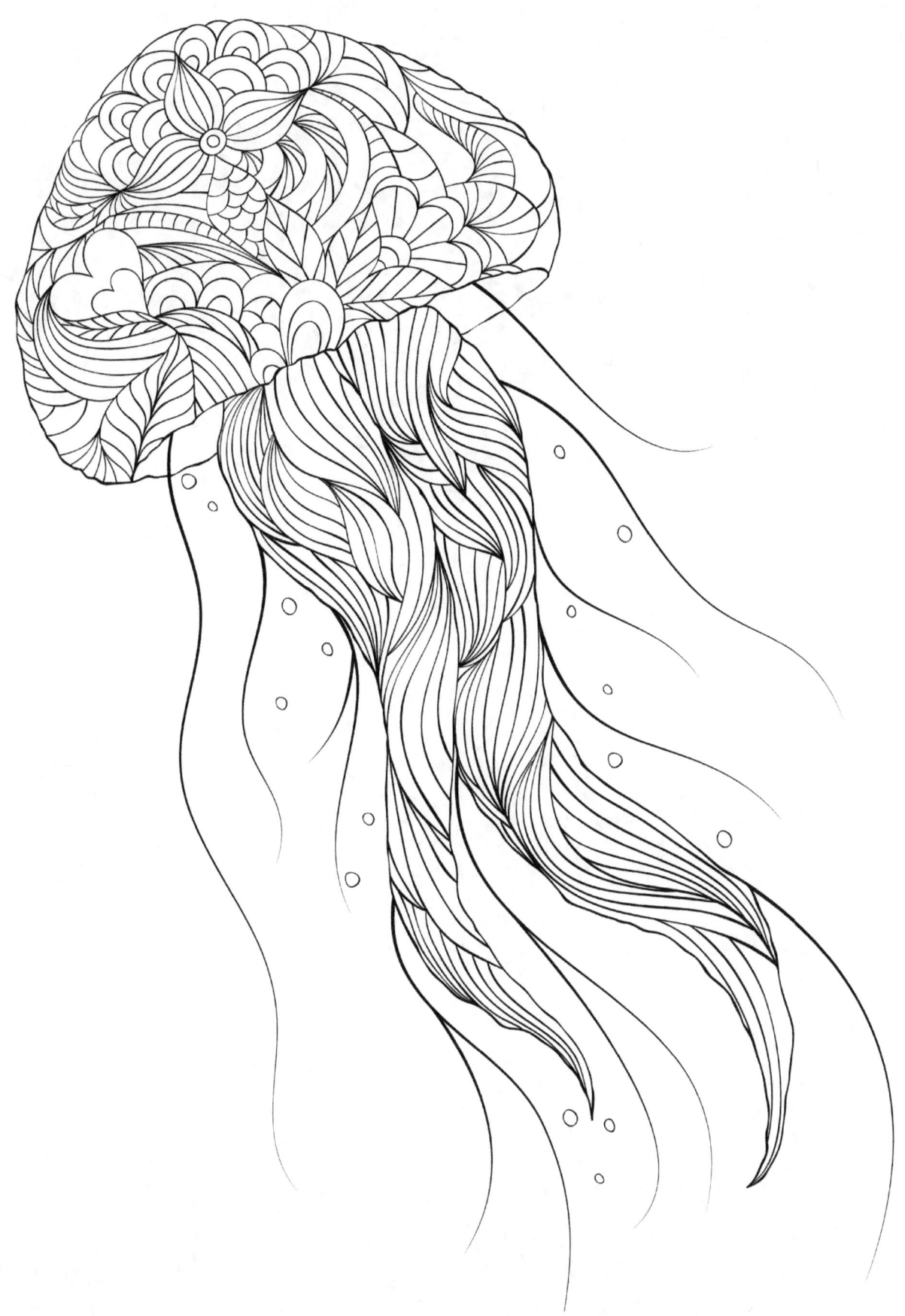

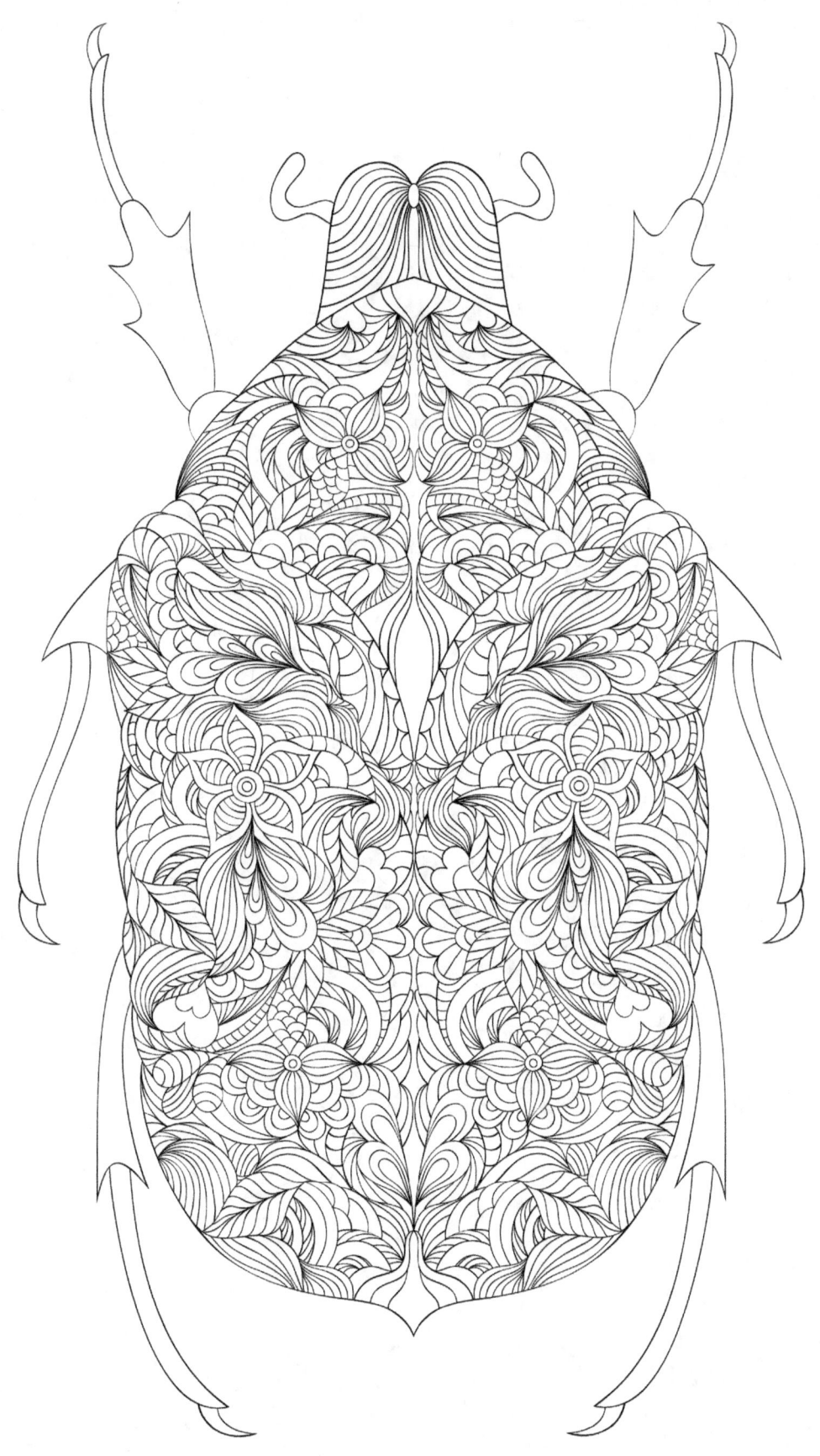

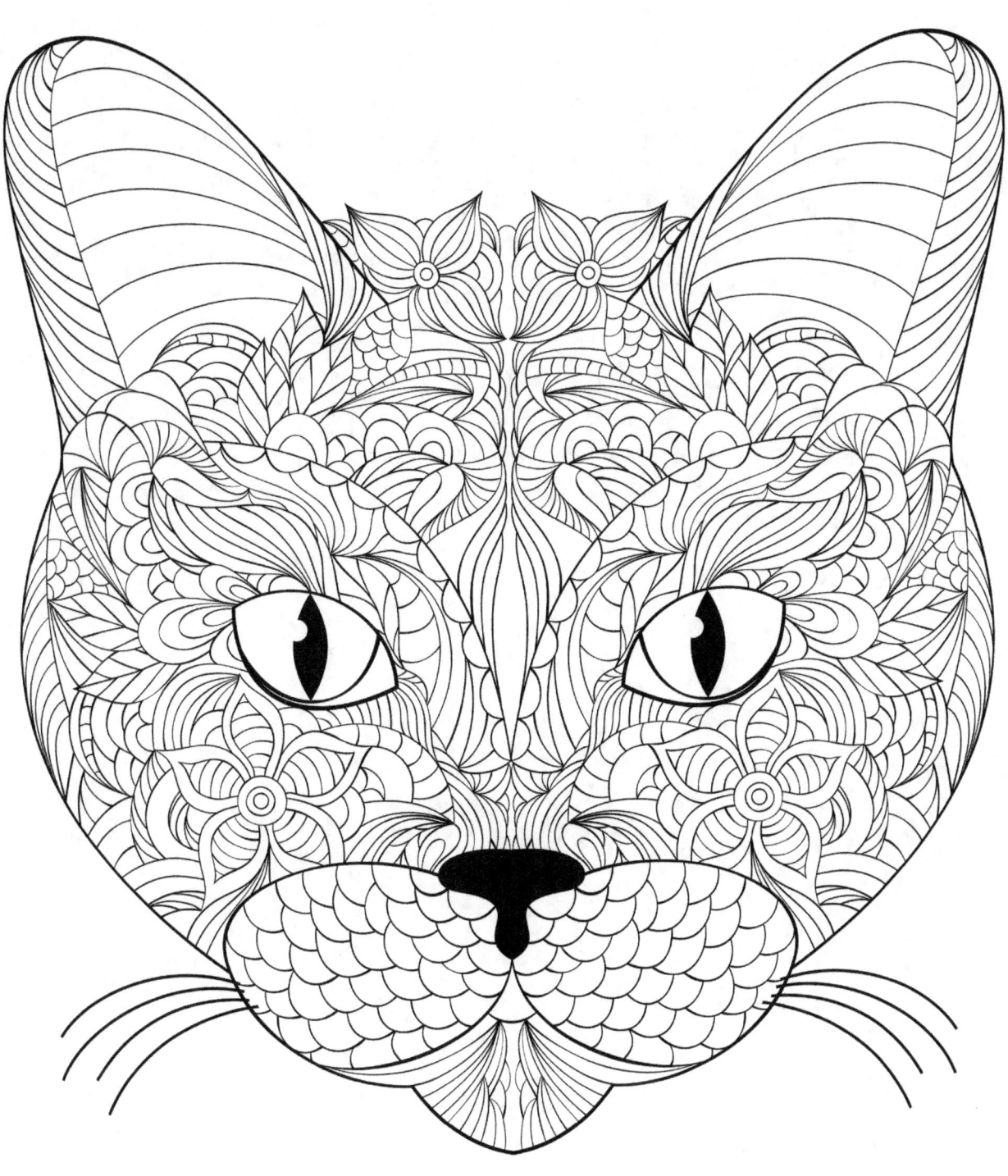

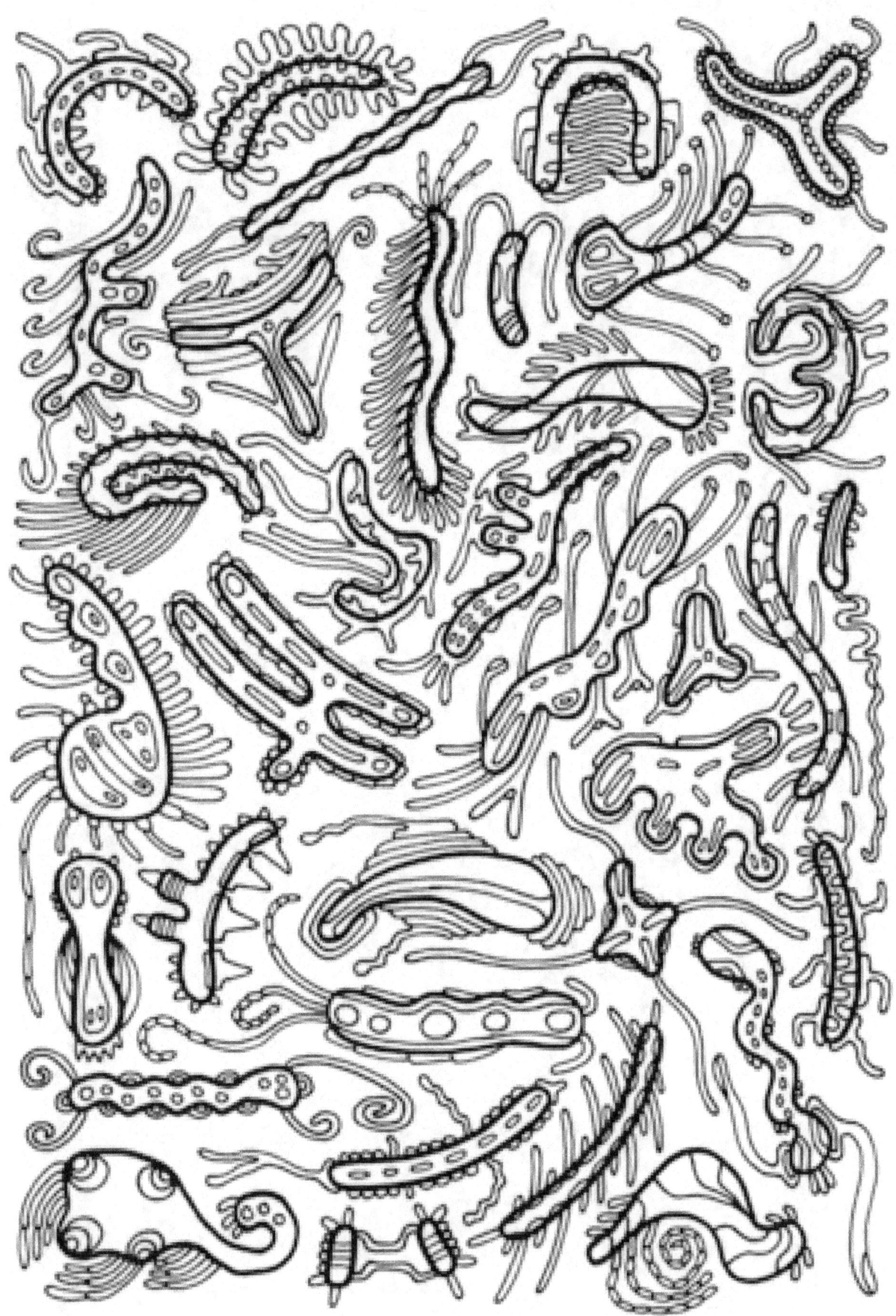

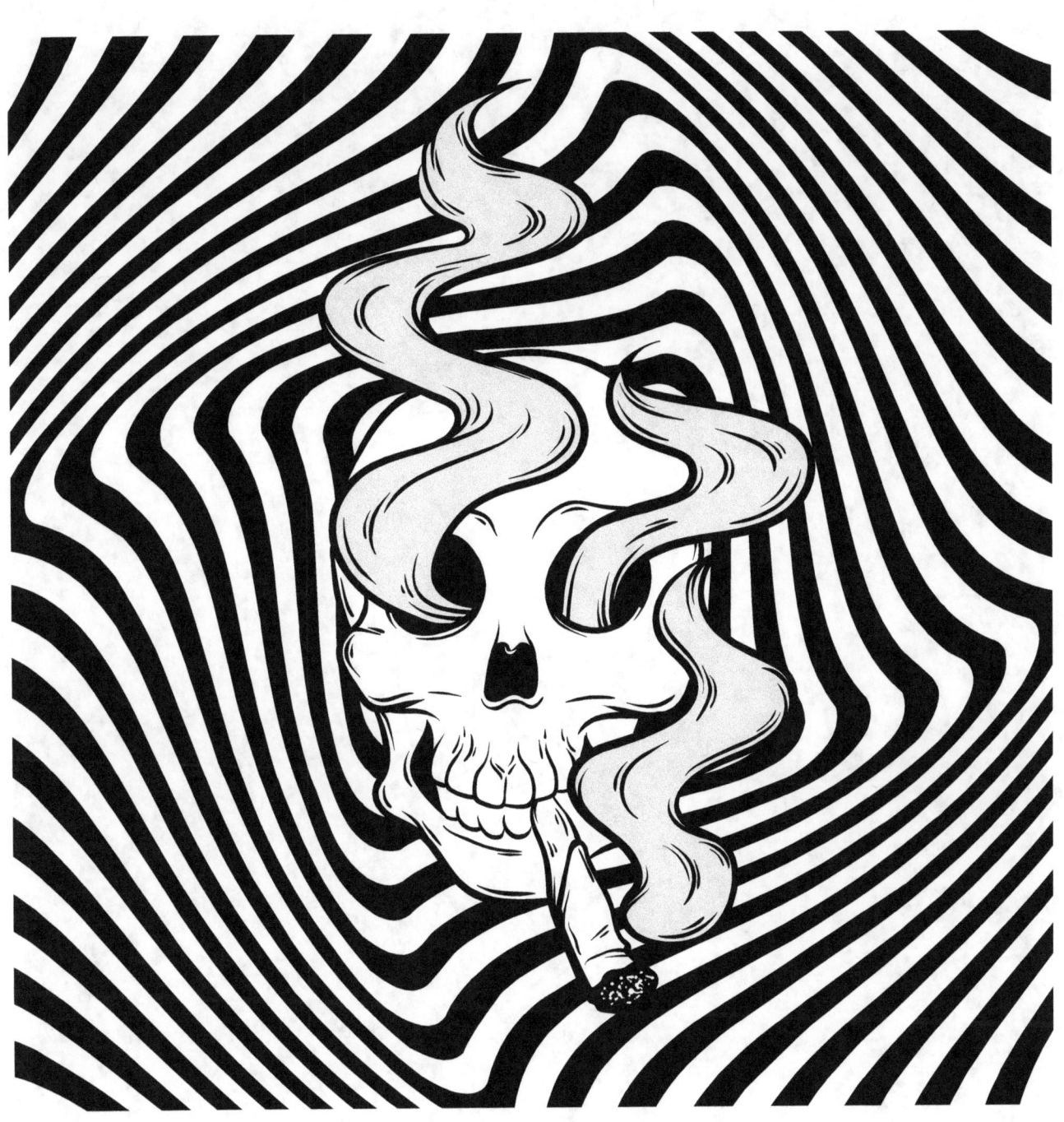

# Think Free Live Free

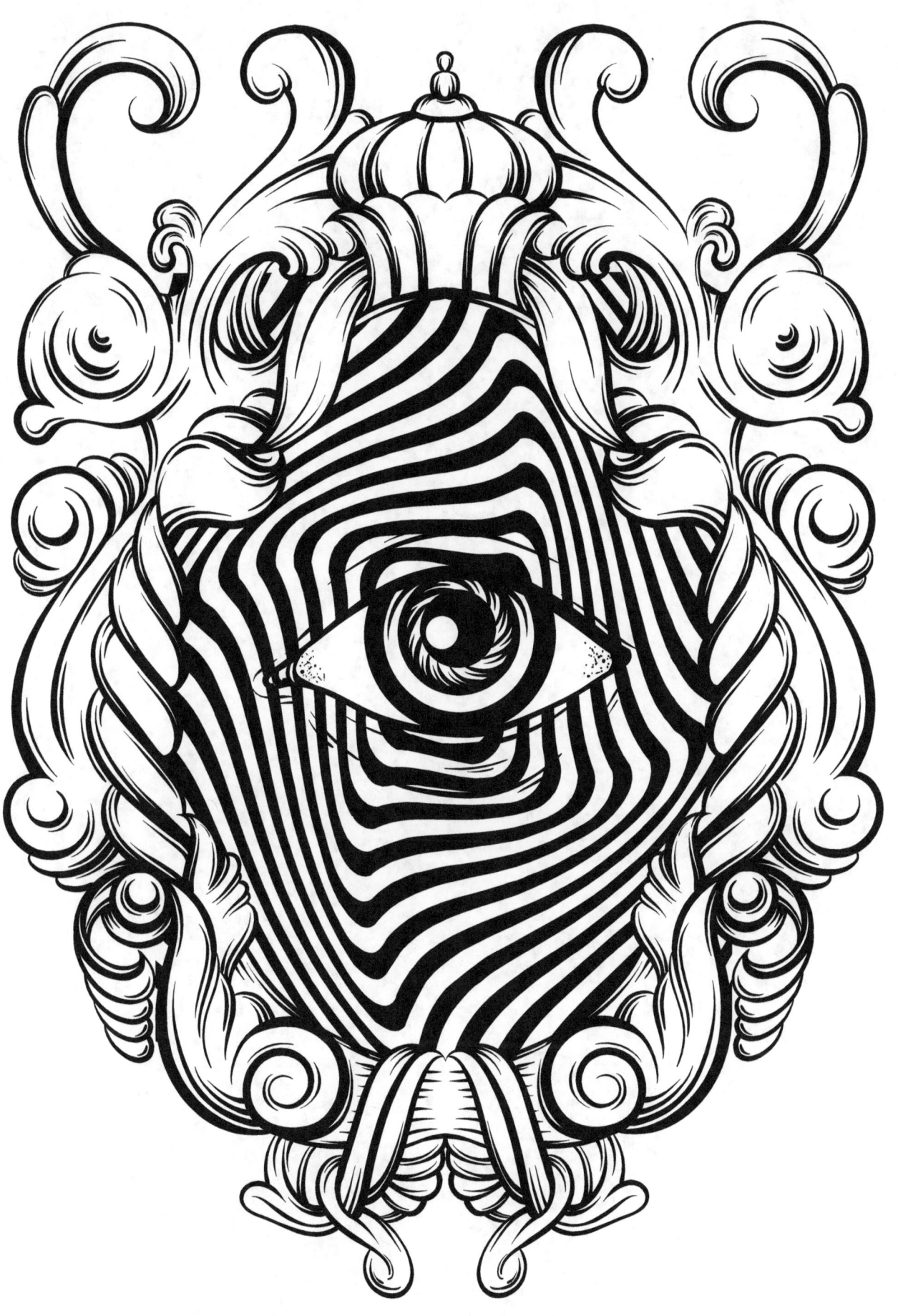

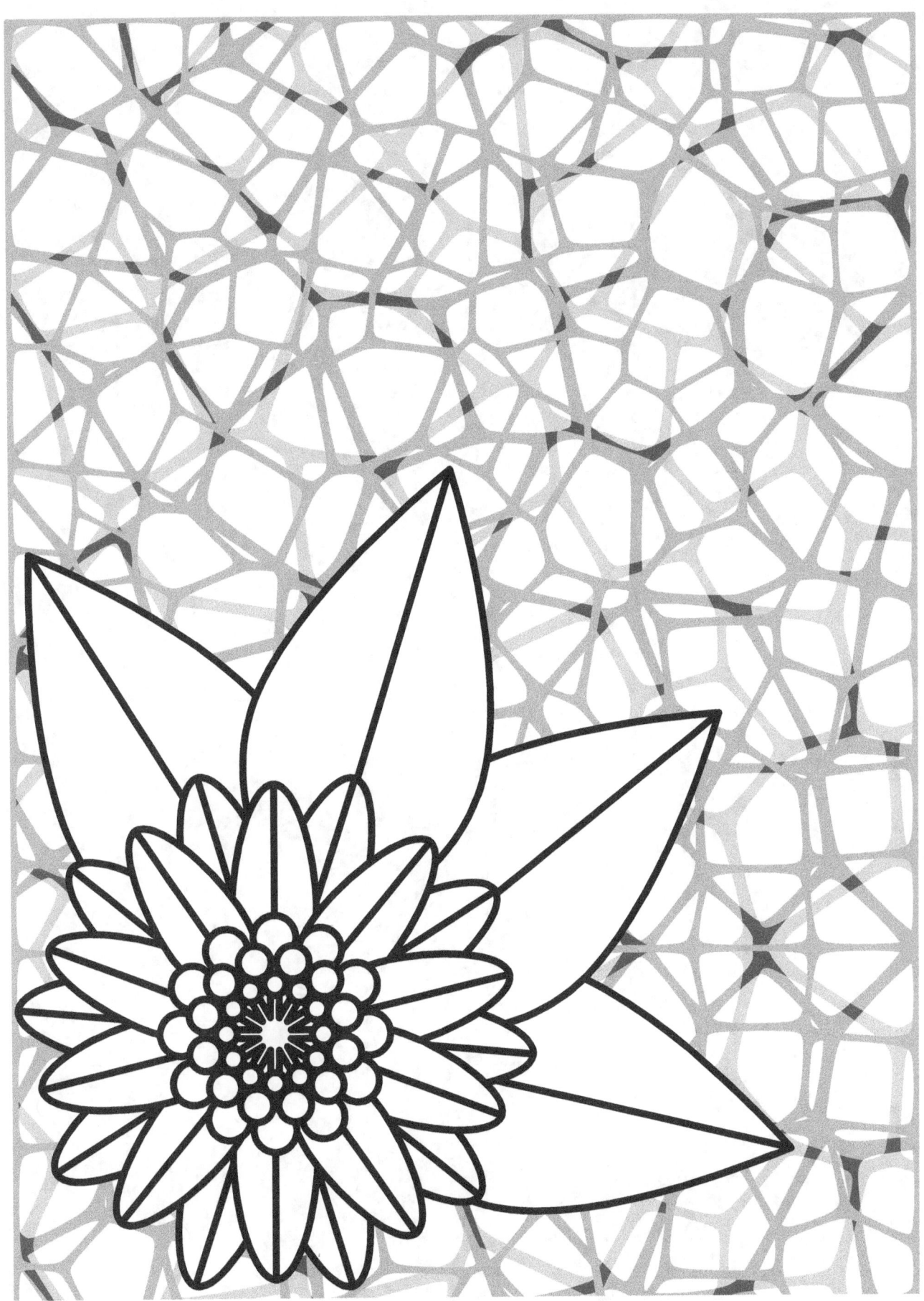

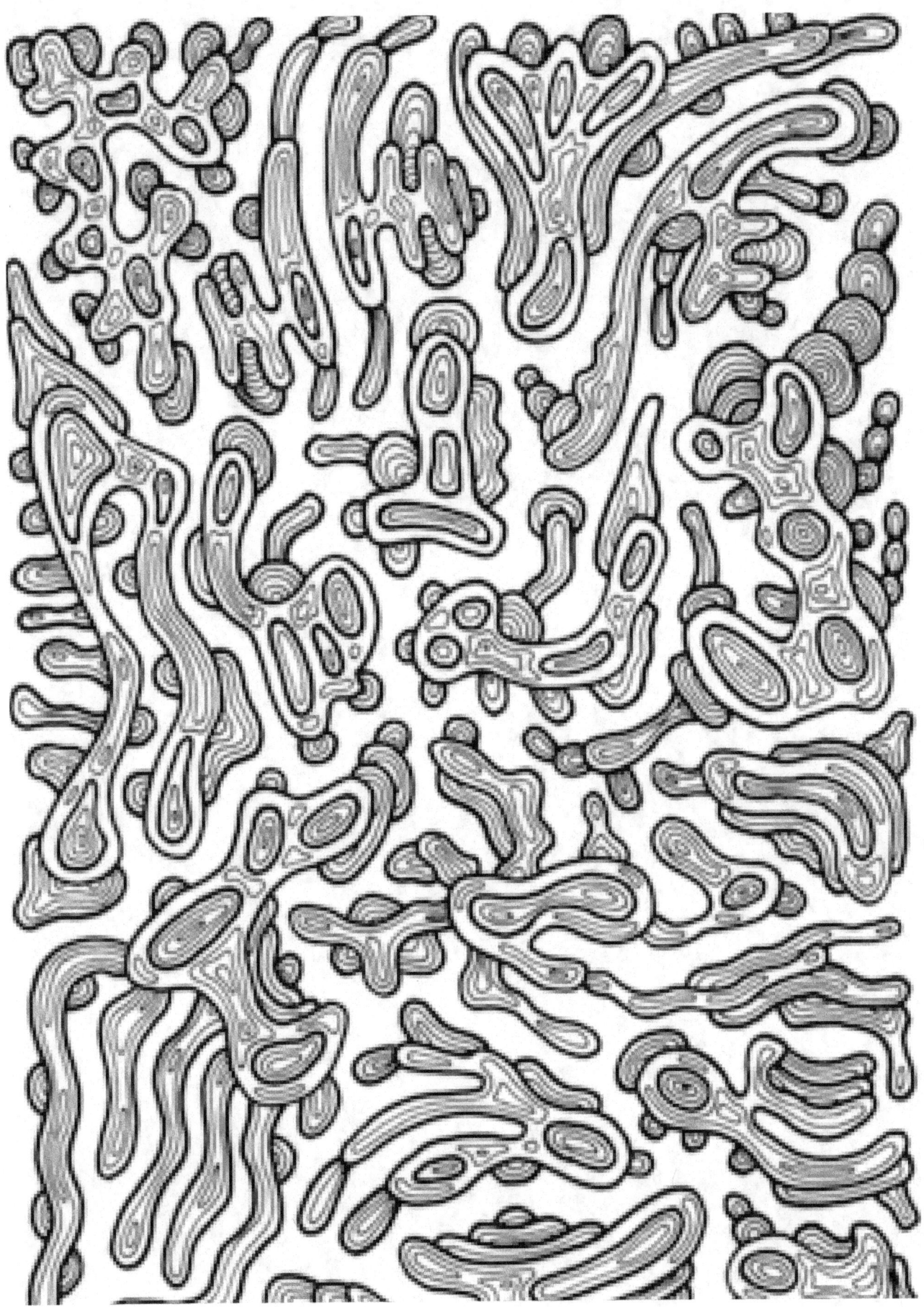

# THE MORE YOU CARE THE MORE YOU LOOSE

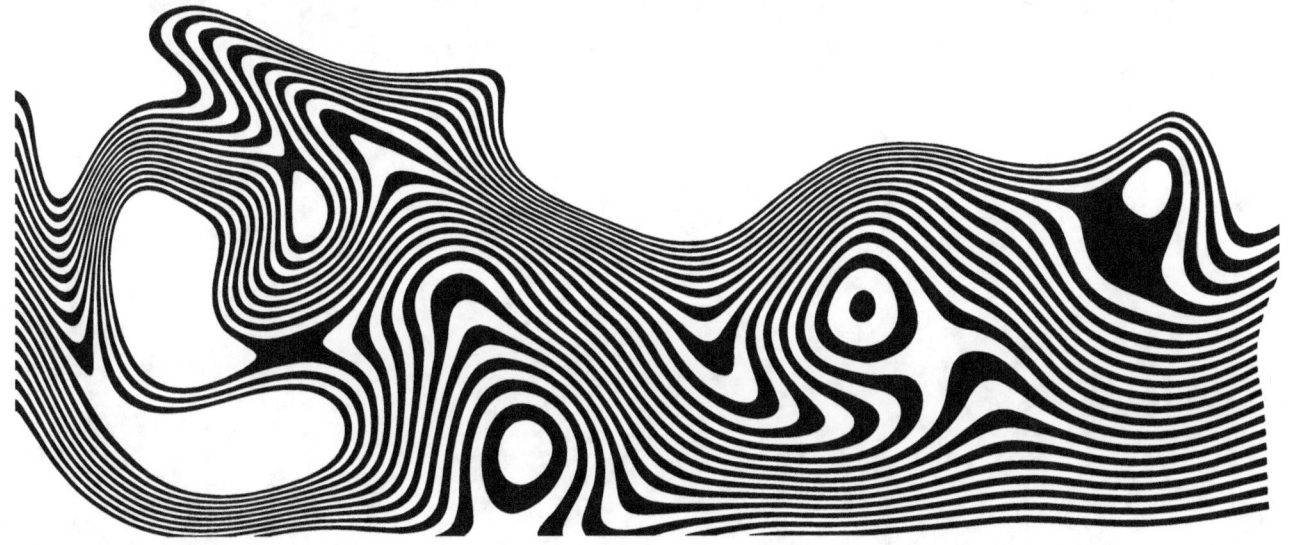

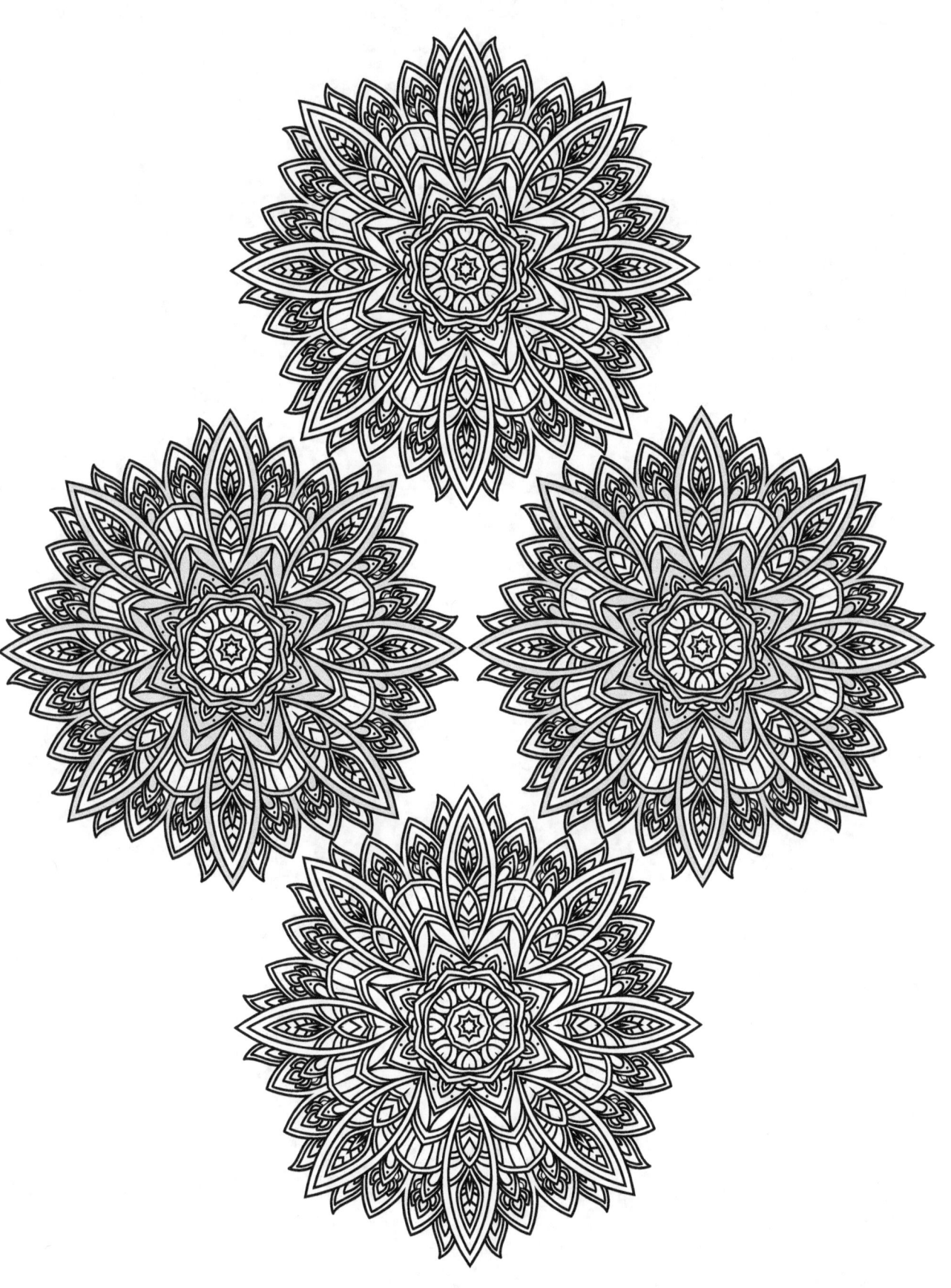

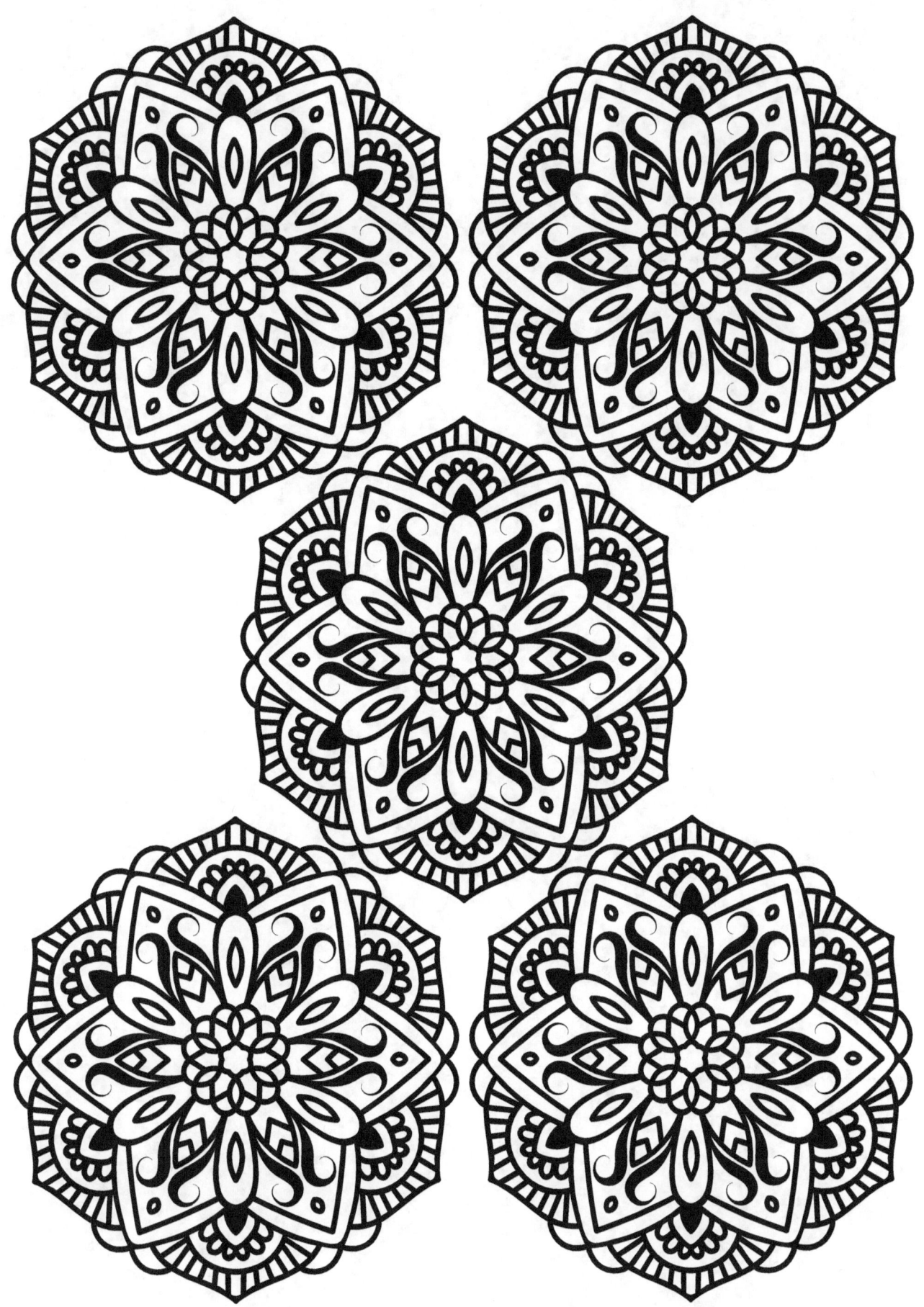

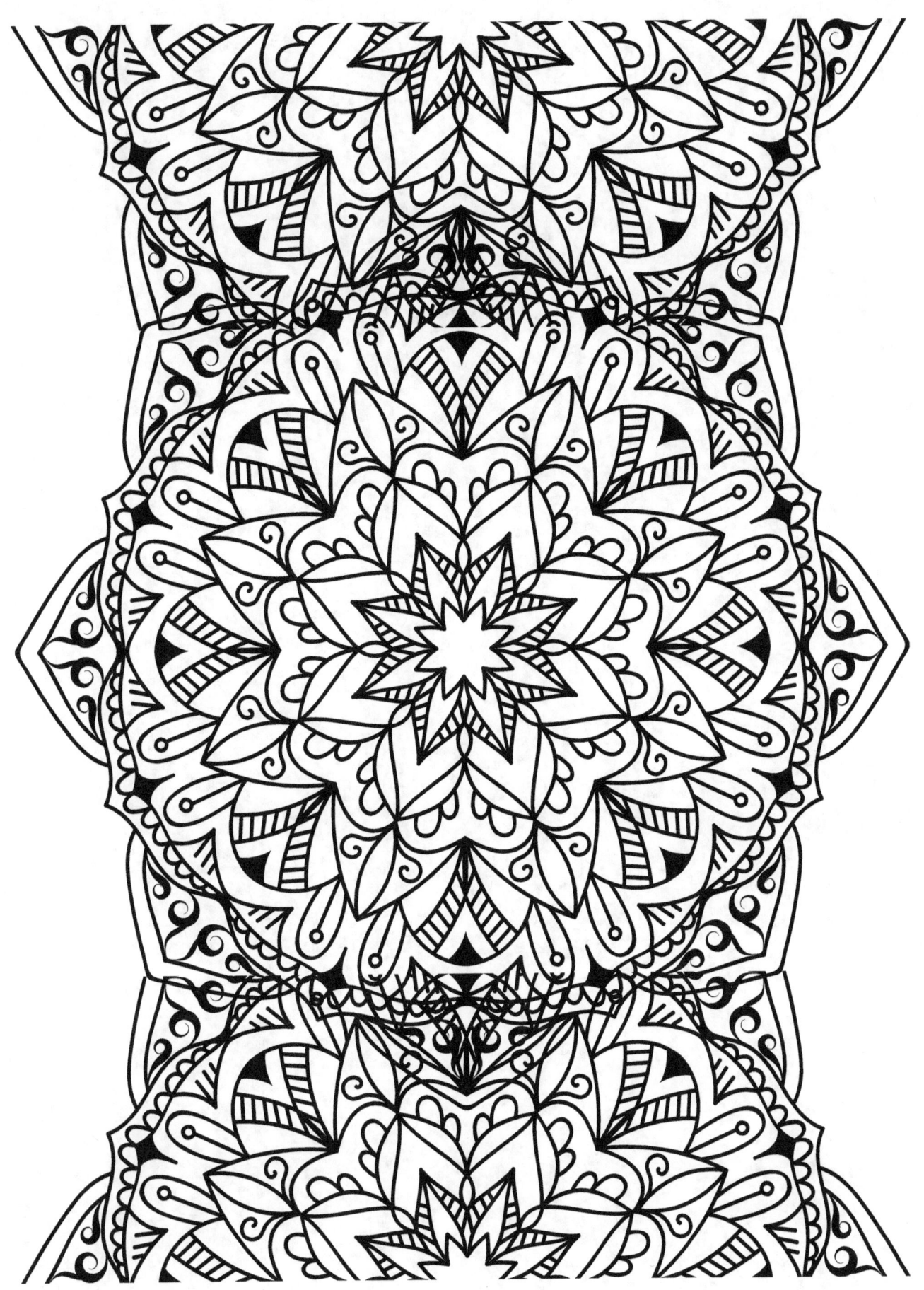

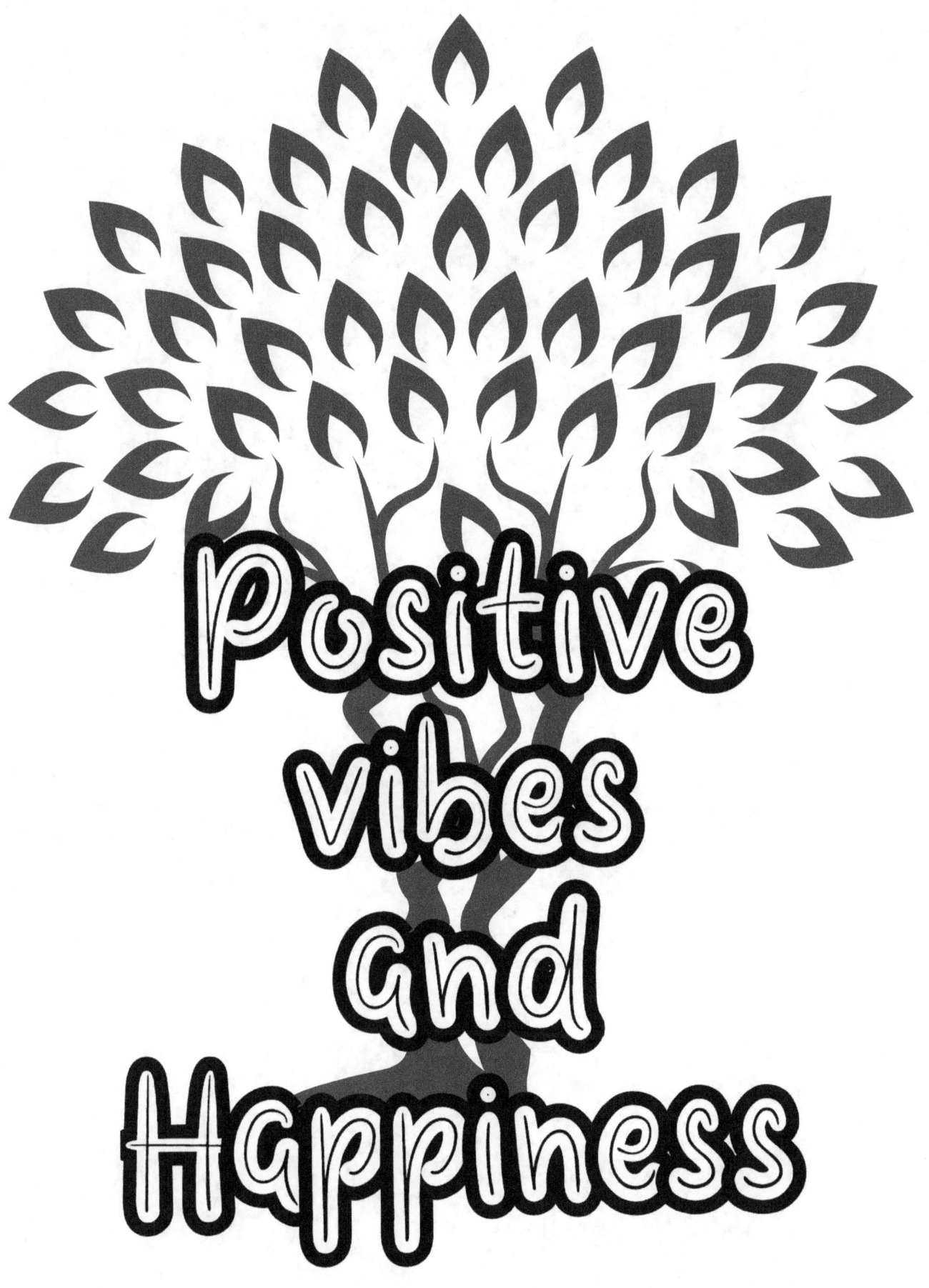

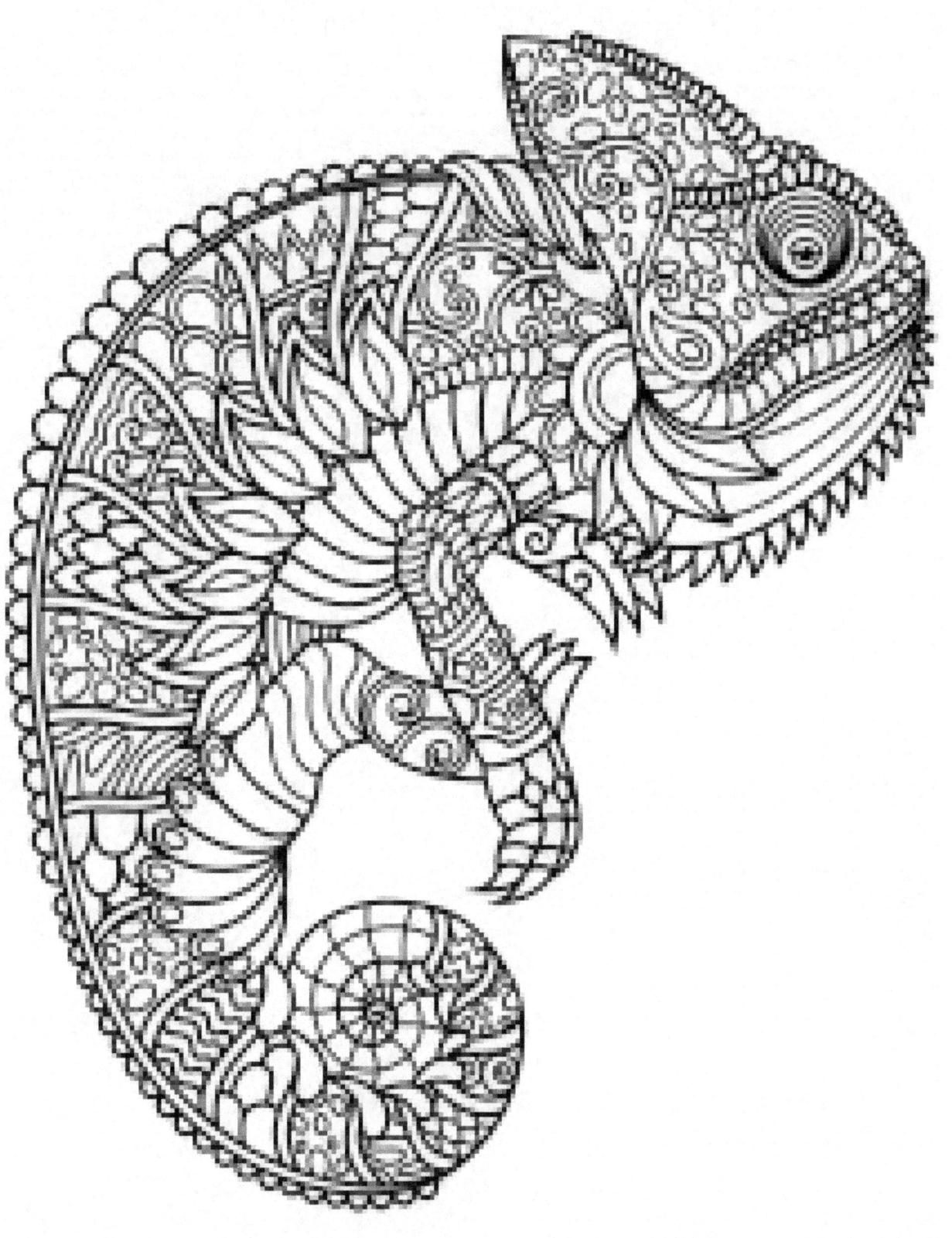

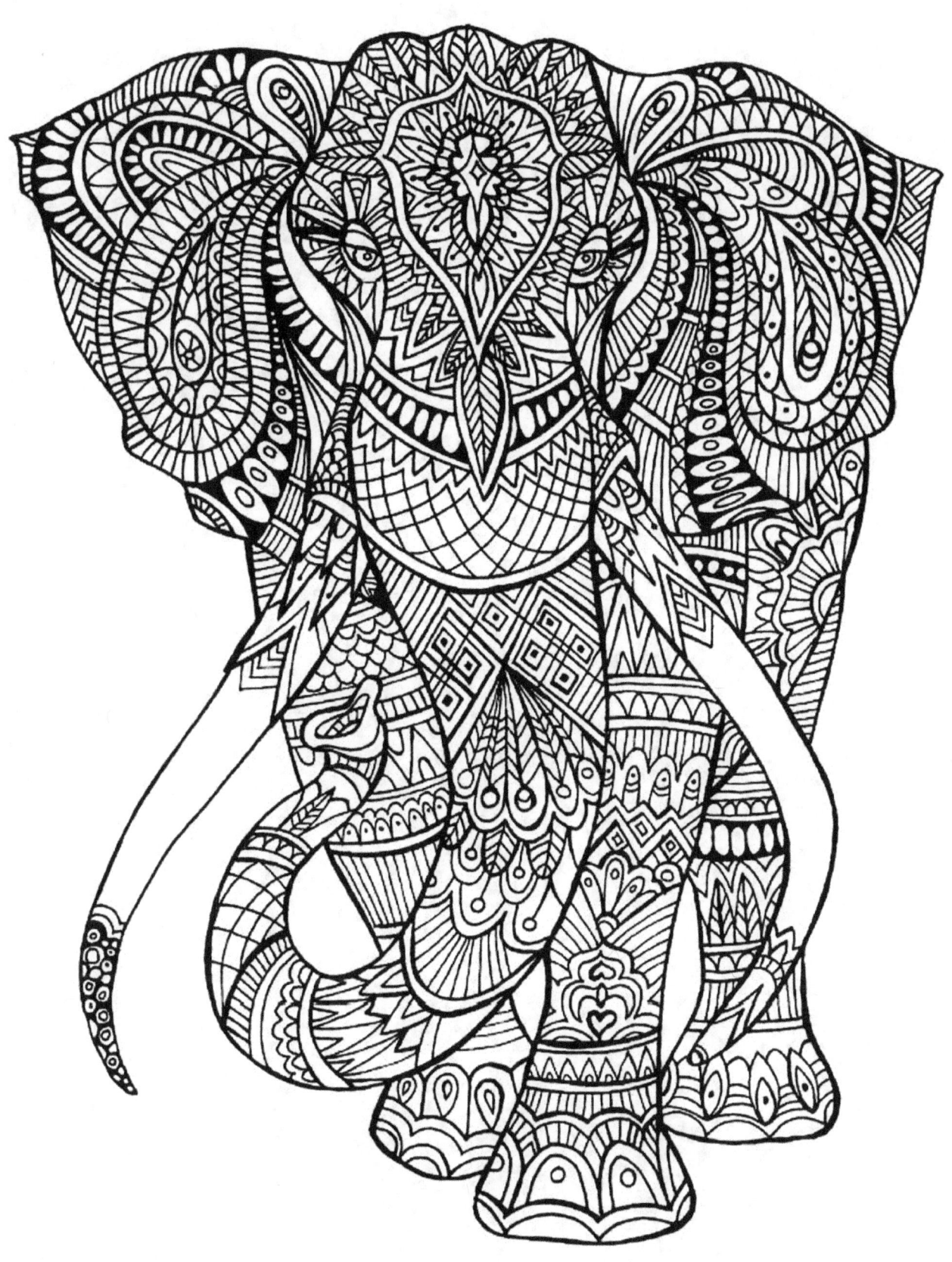

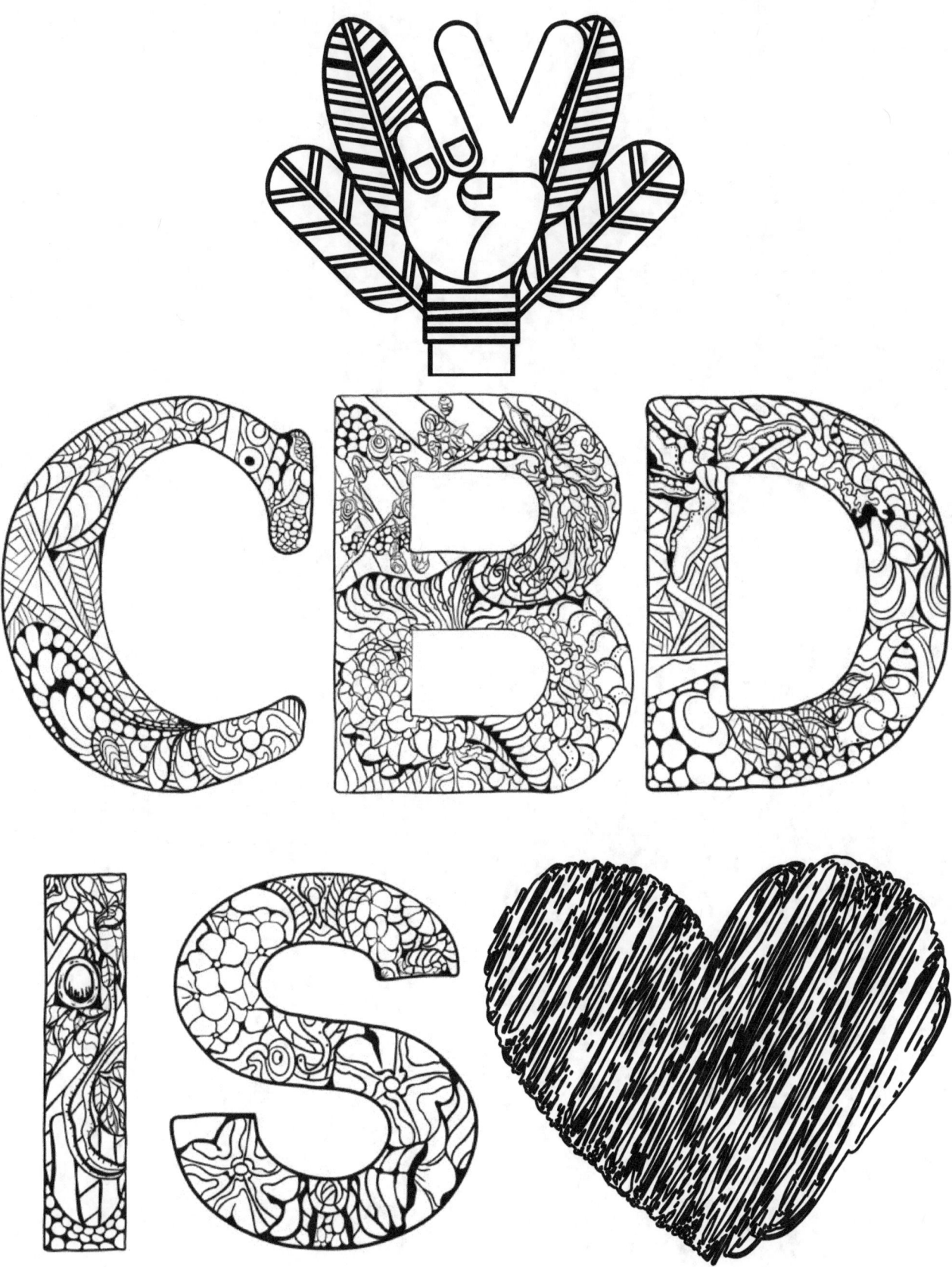

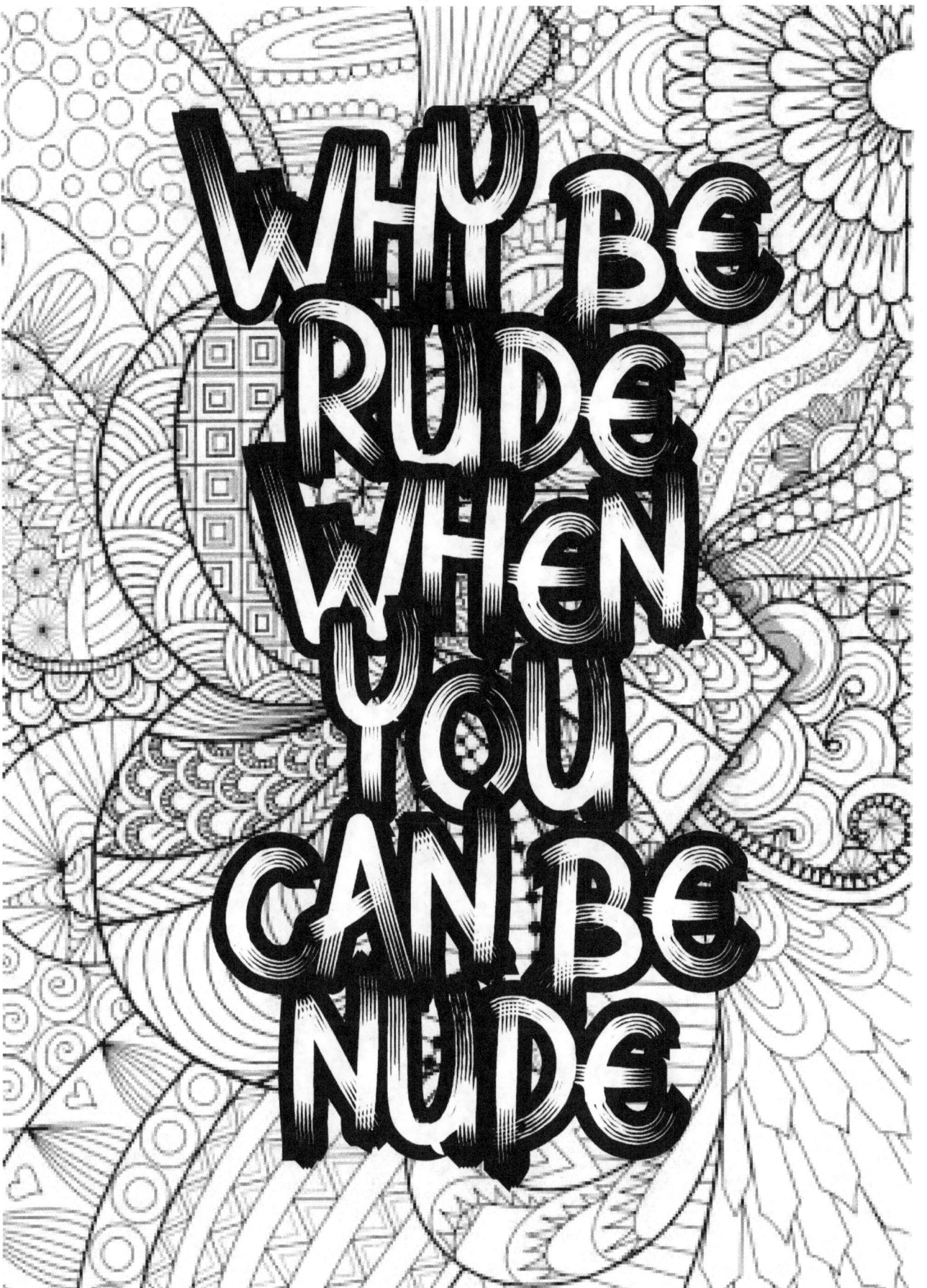

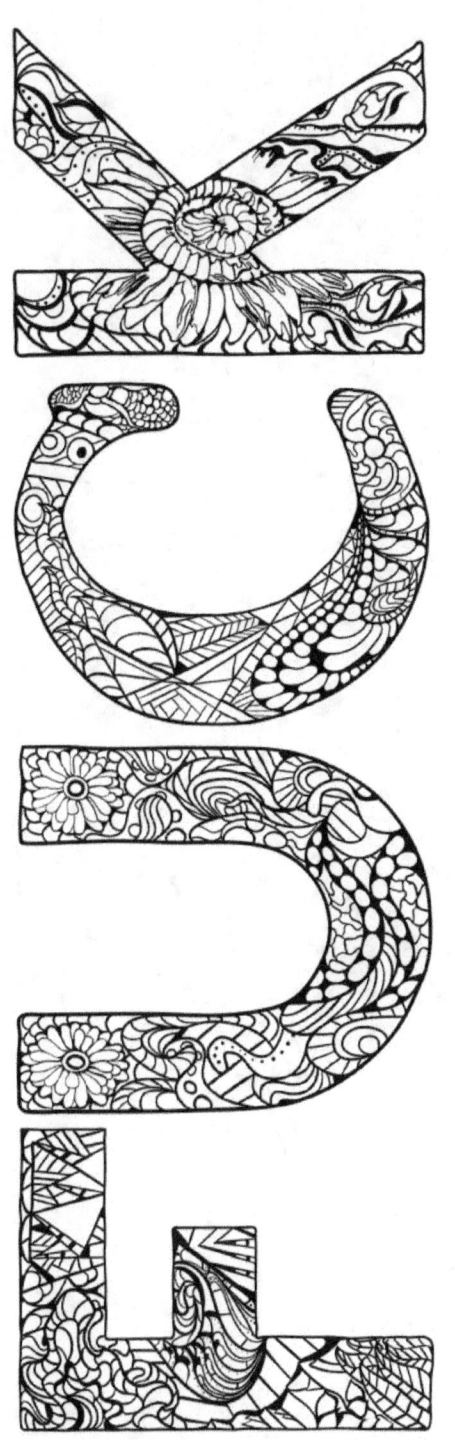
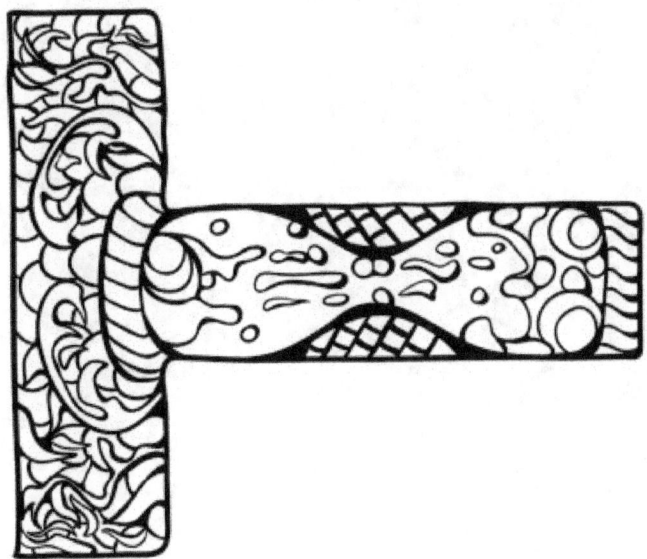
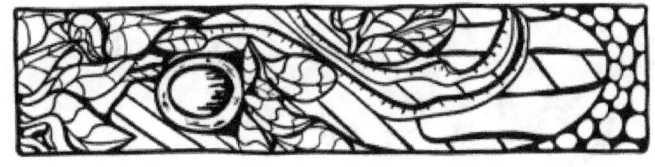

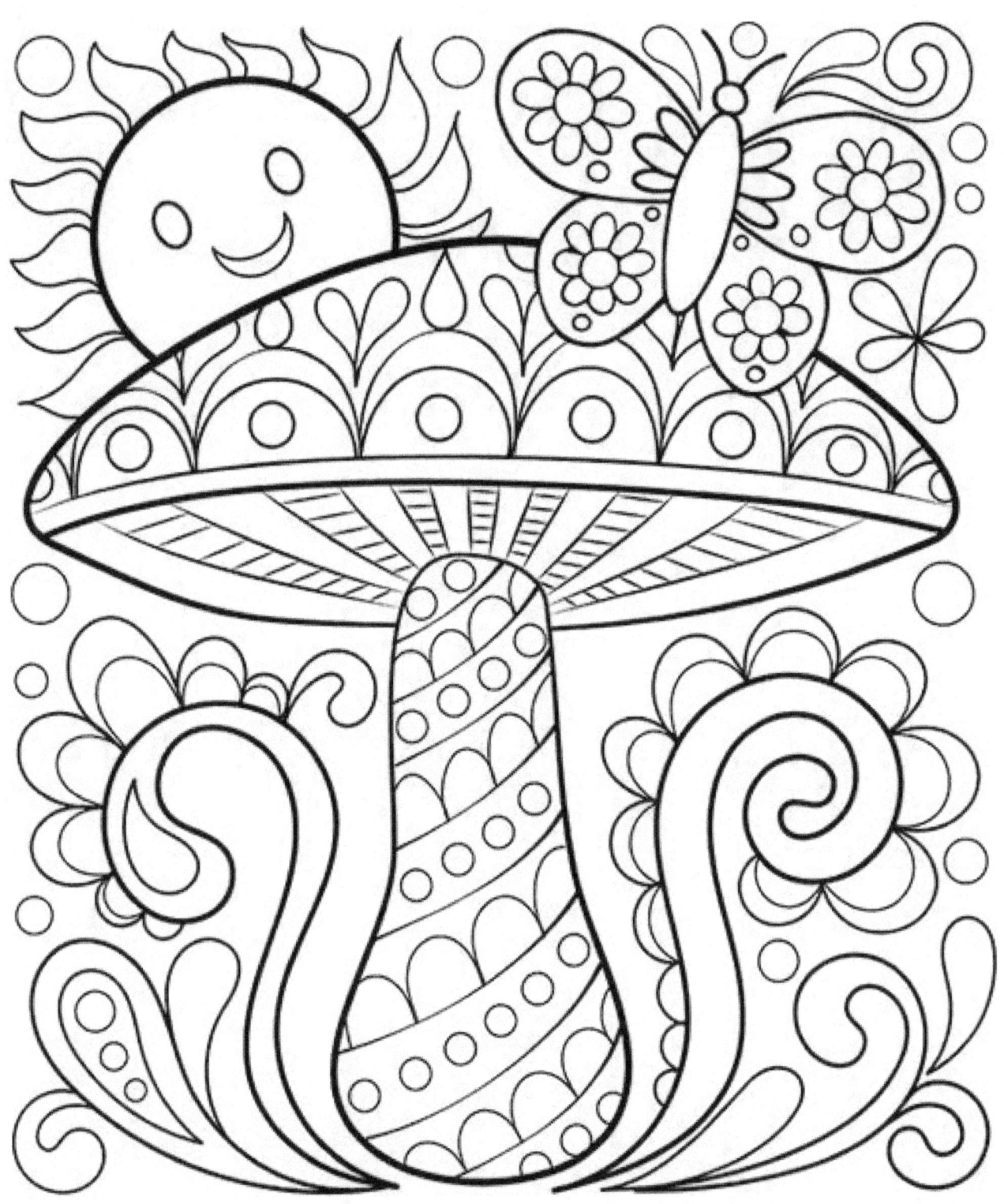

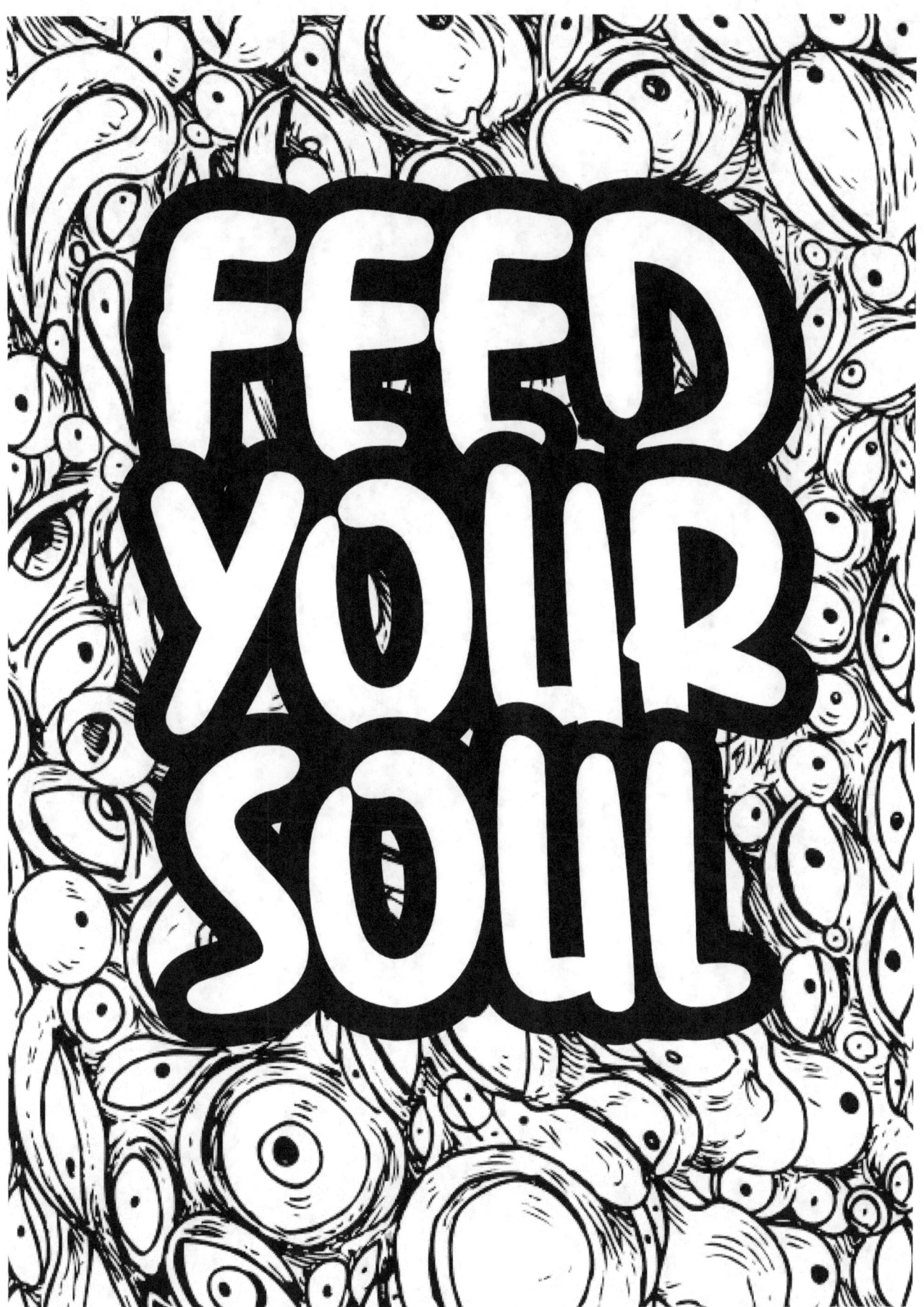

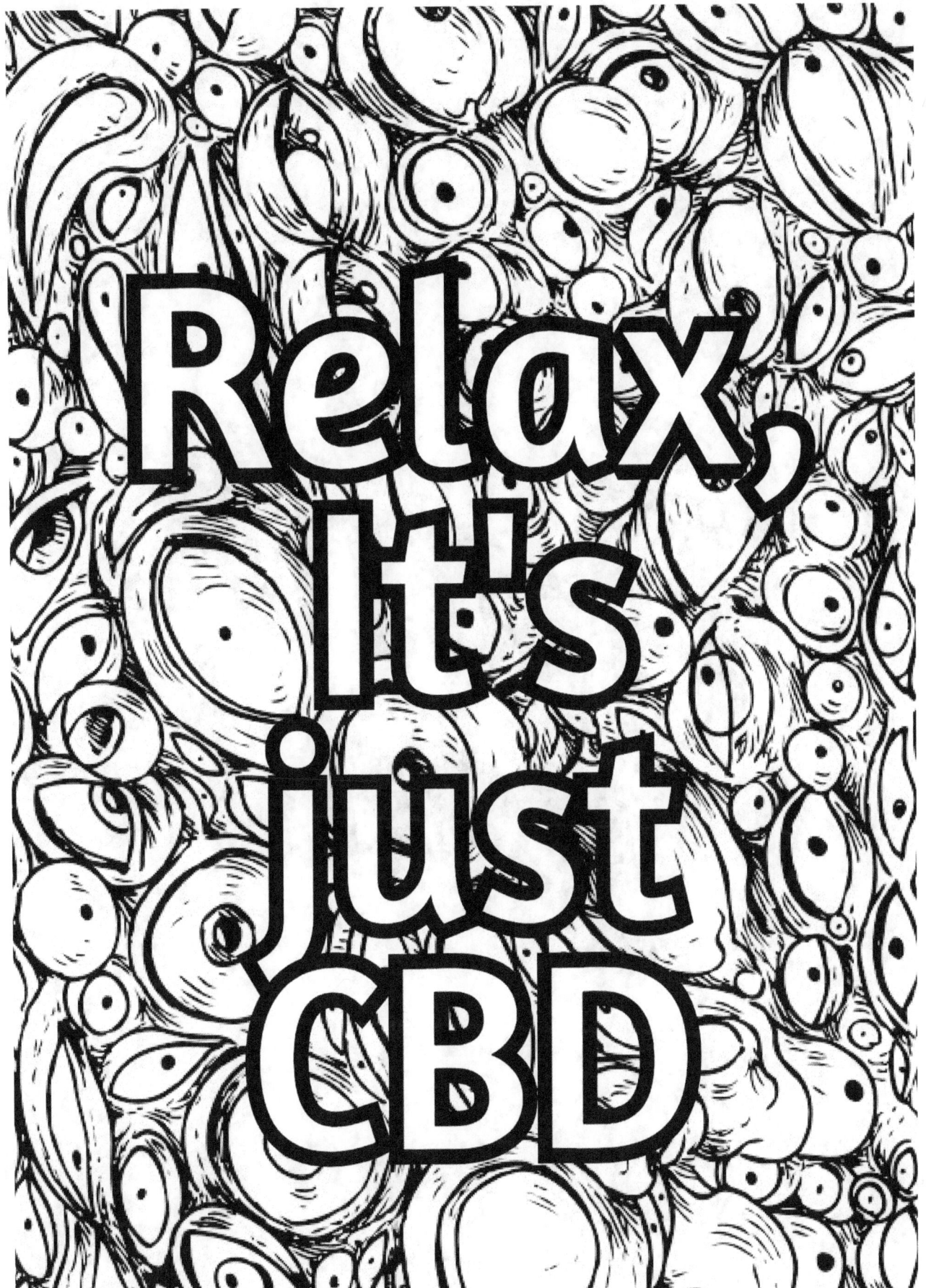

Thank you!

www.ingramcontent.com/pod-product-compliance
Lightning Source LLC
Chambersburg PA
CBHW081057240526
45465CB00025B/2456